Cars Coloring Book For Kids Ages 6-12

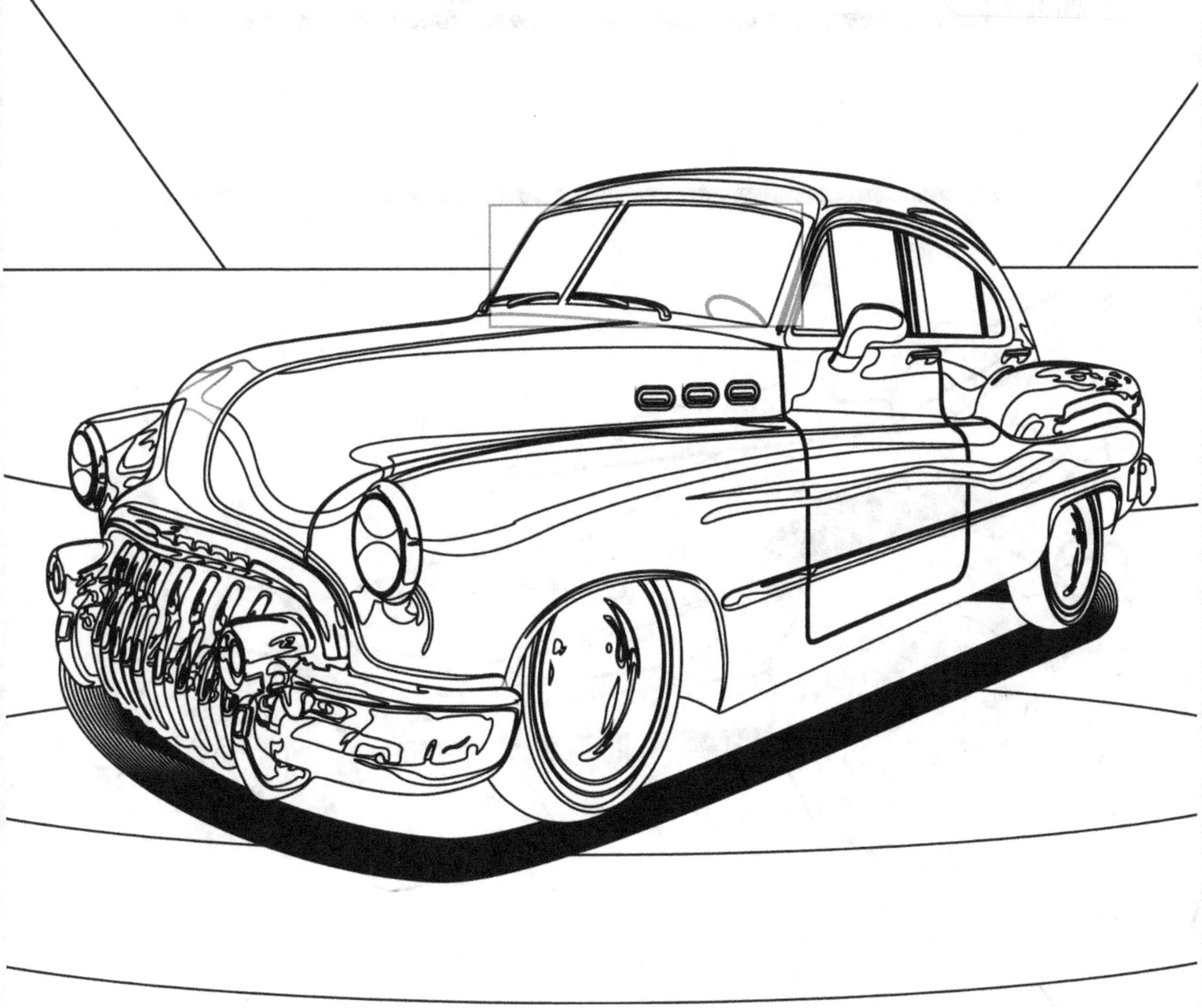

THIS BOOK BELONGS TO

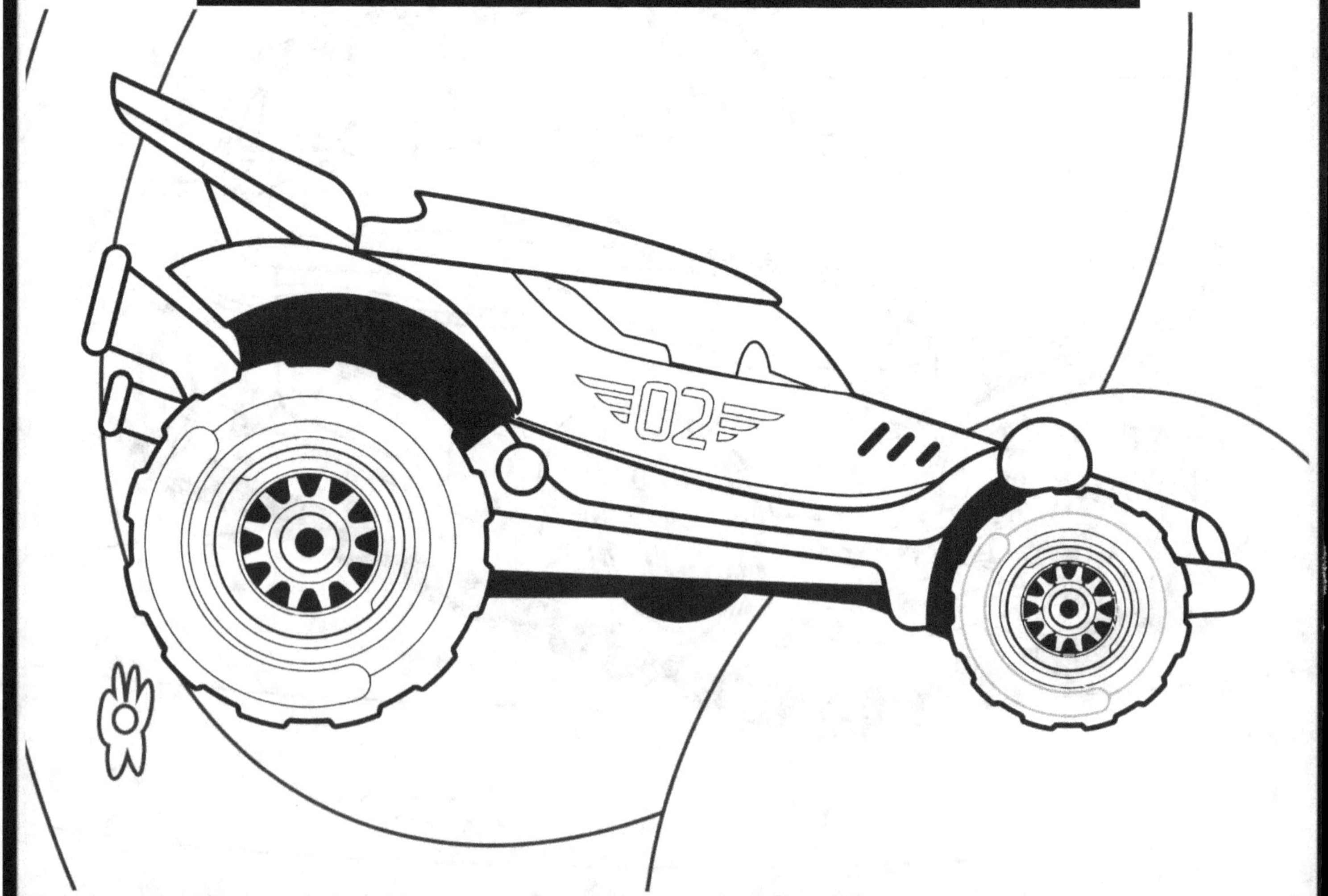

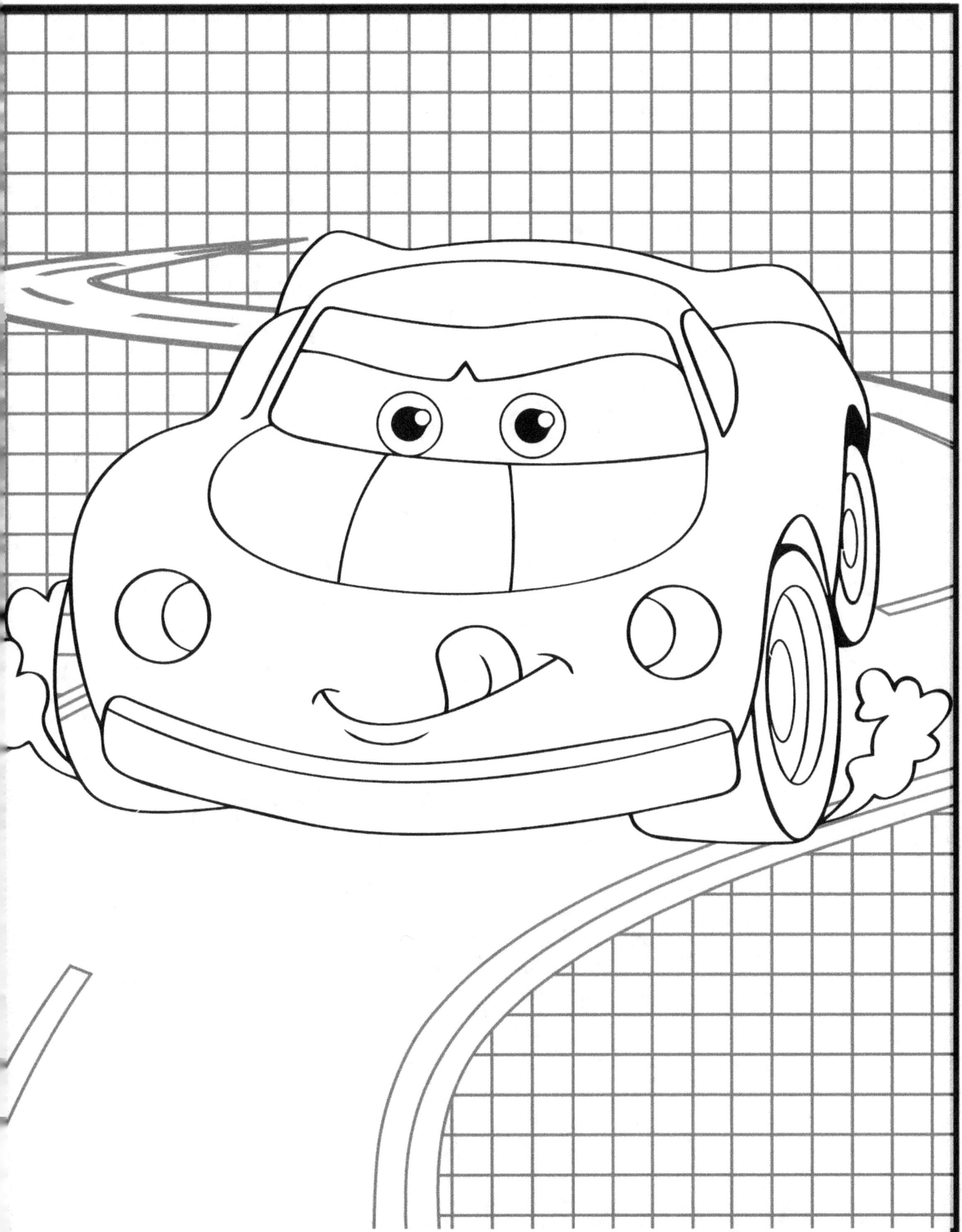

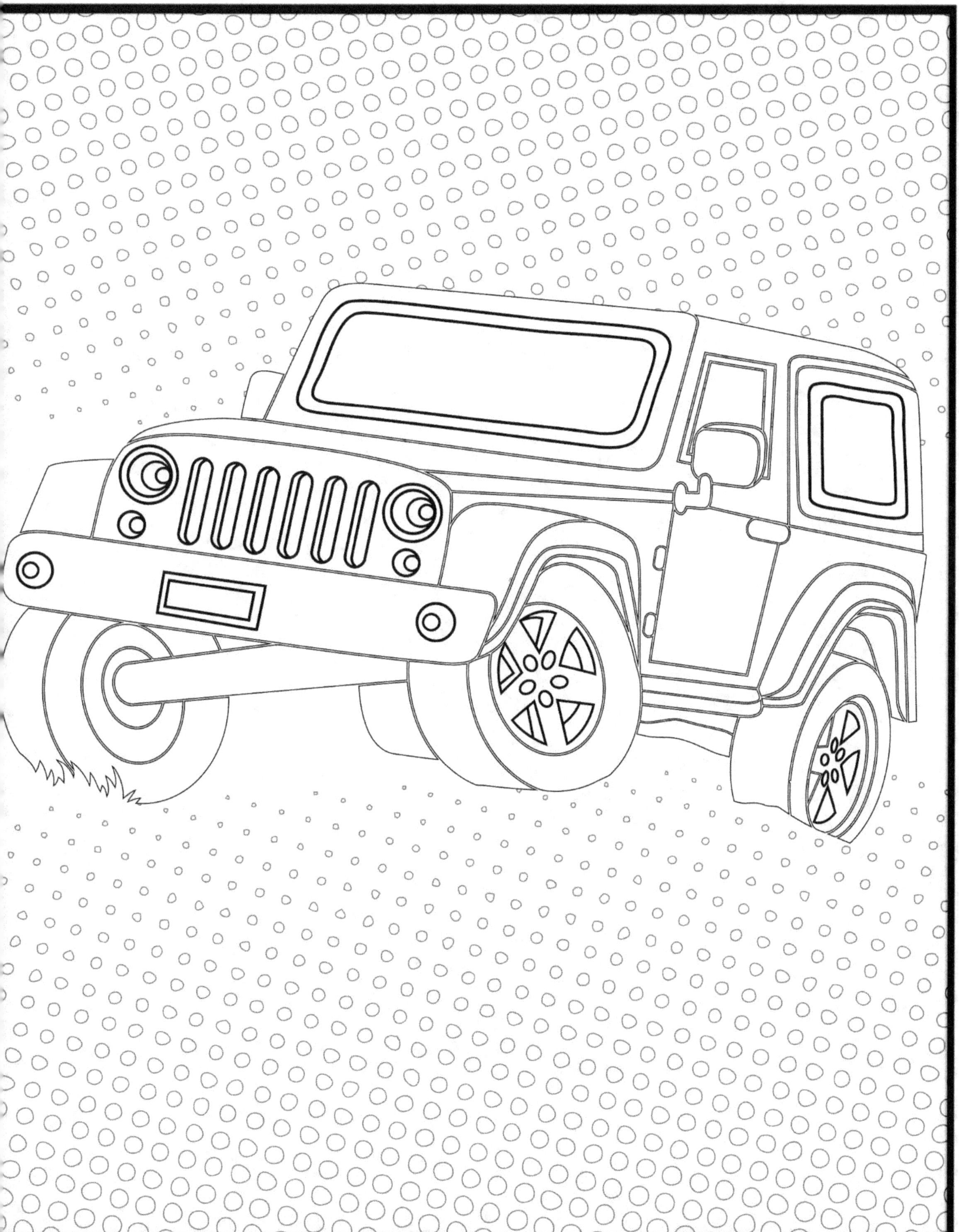

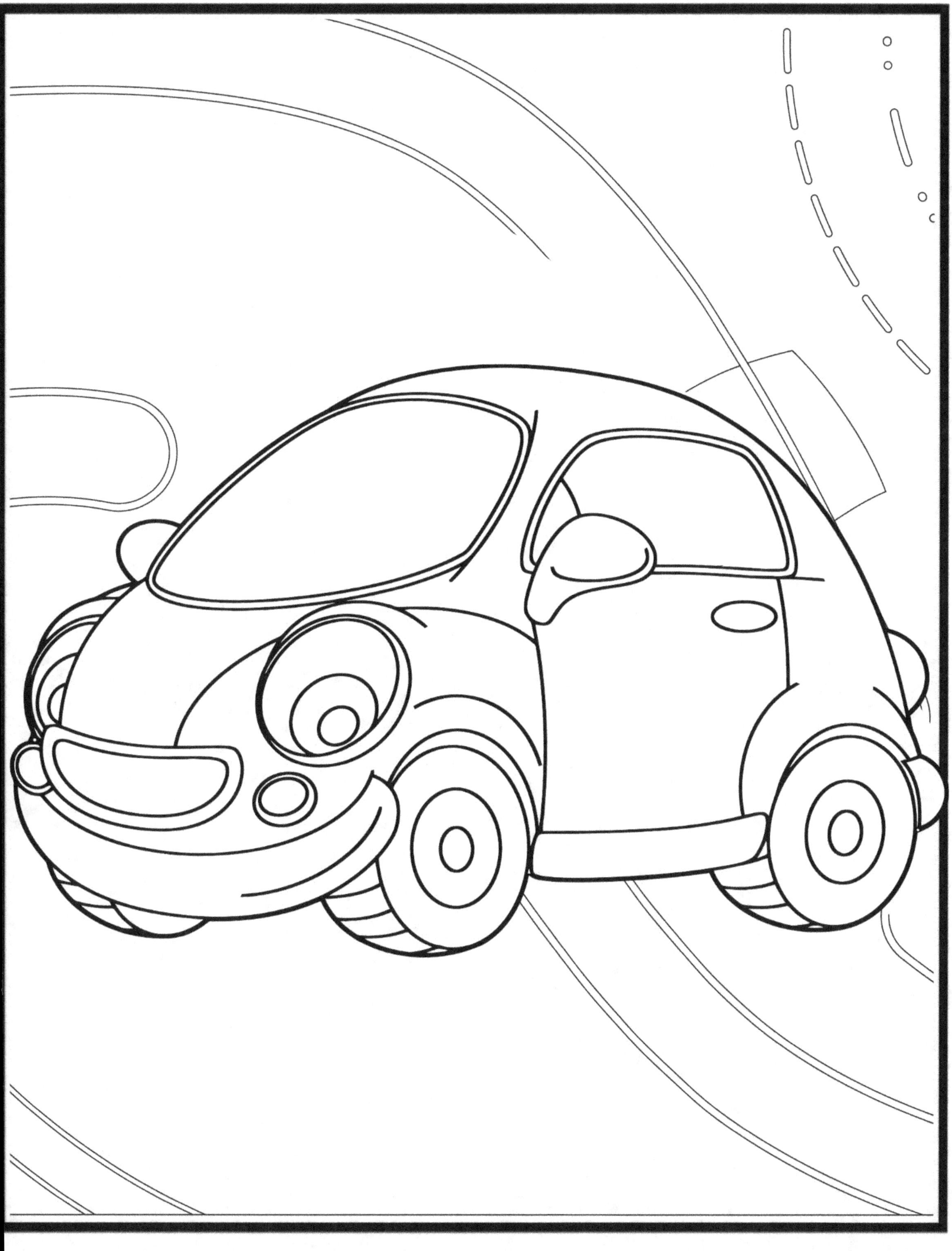

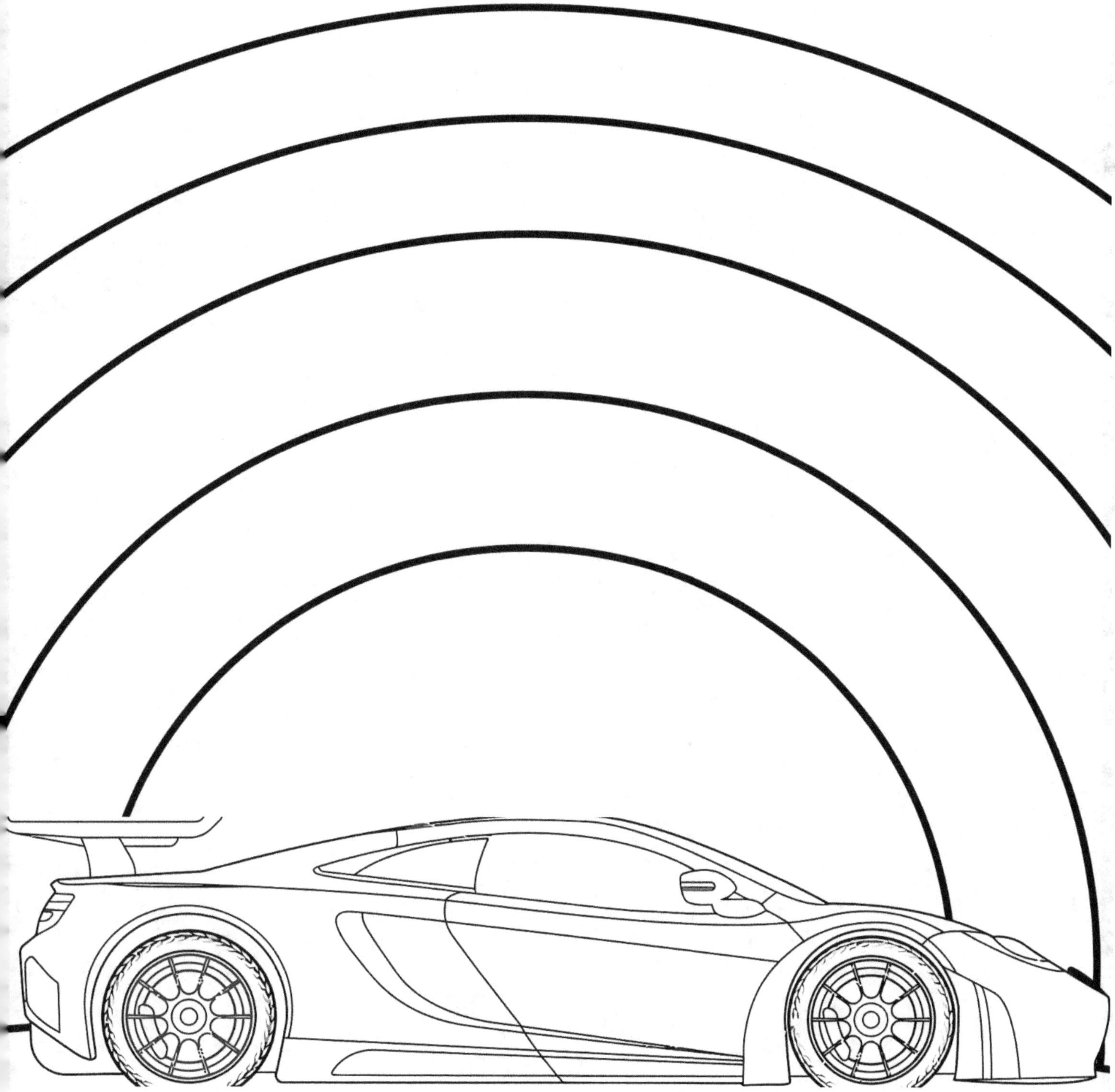

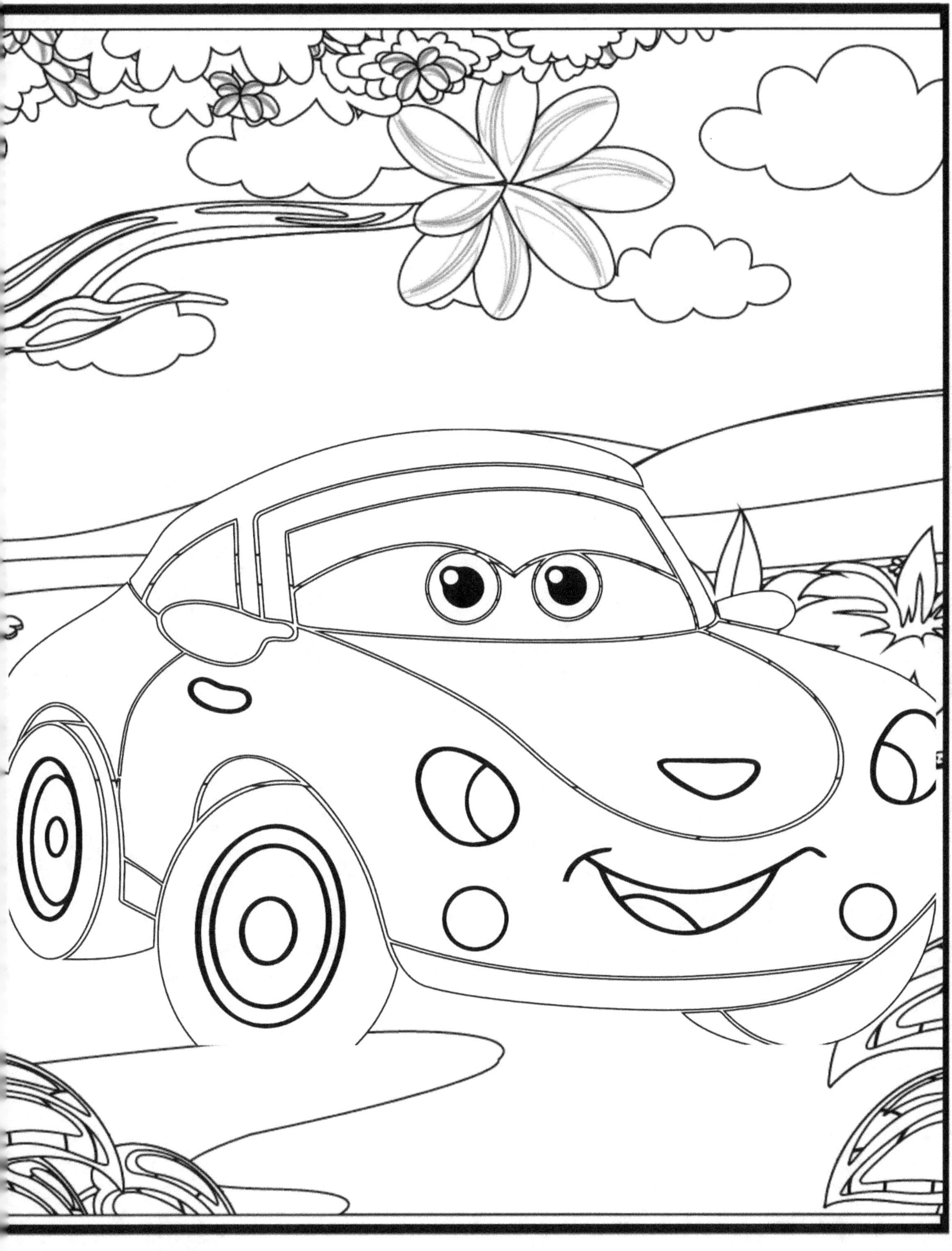

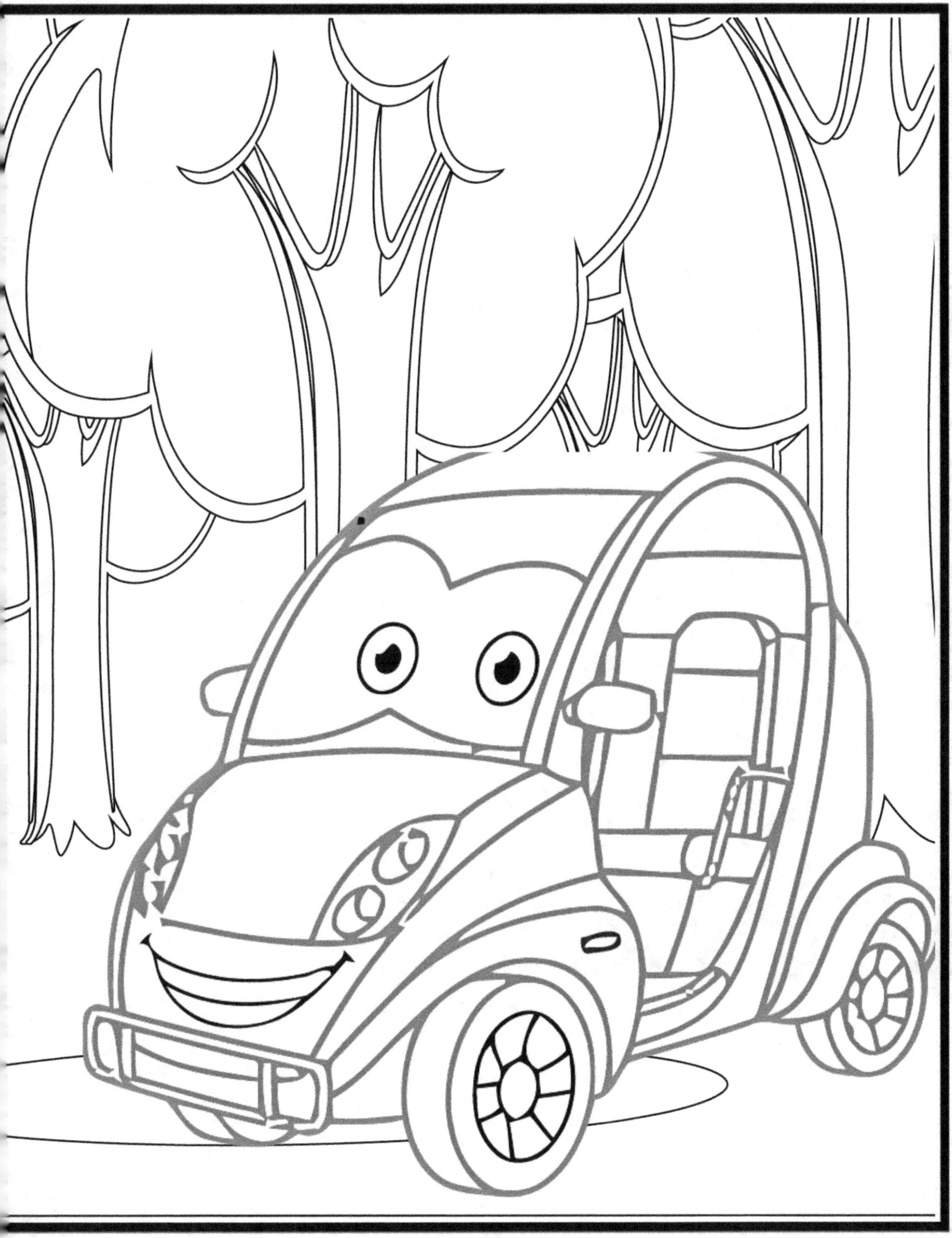

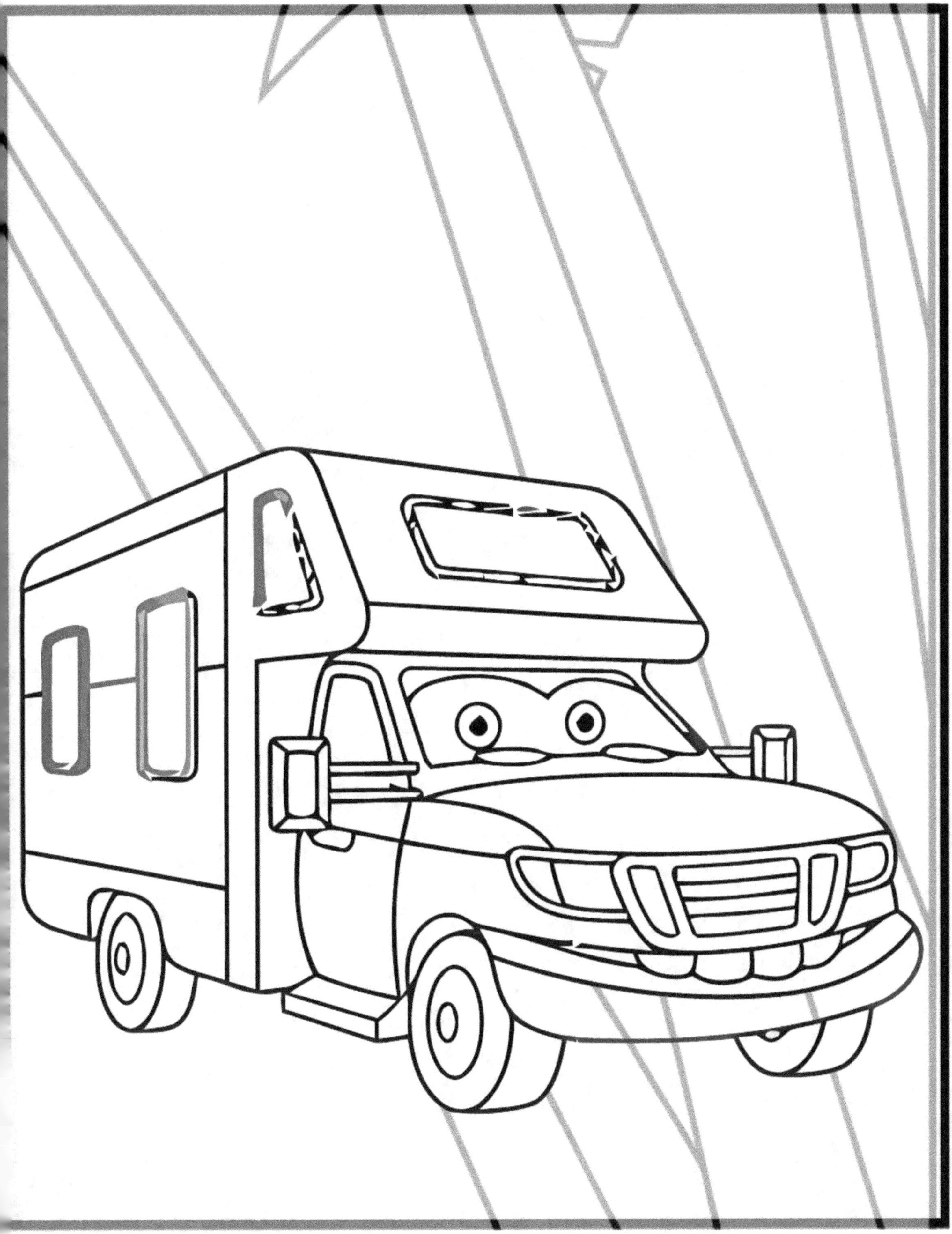

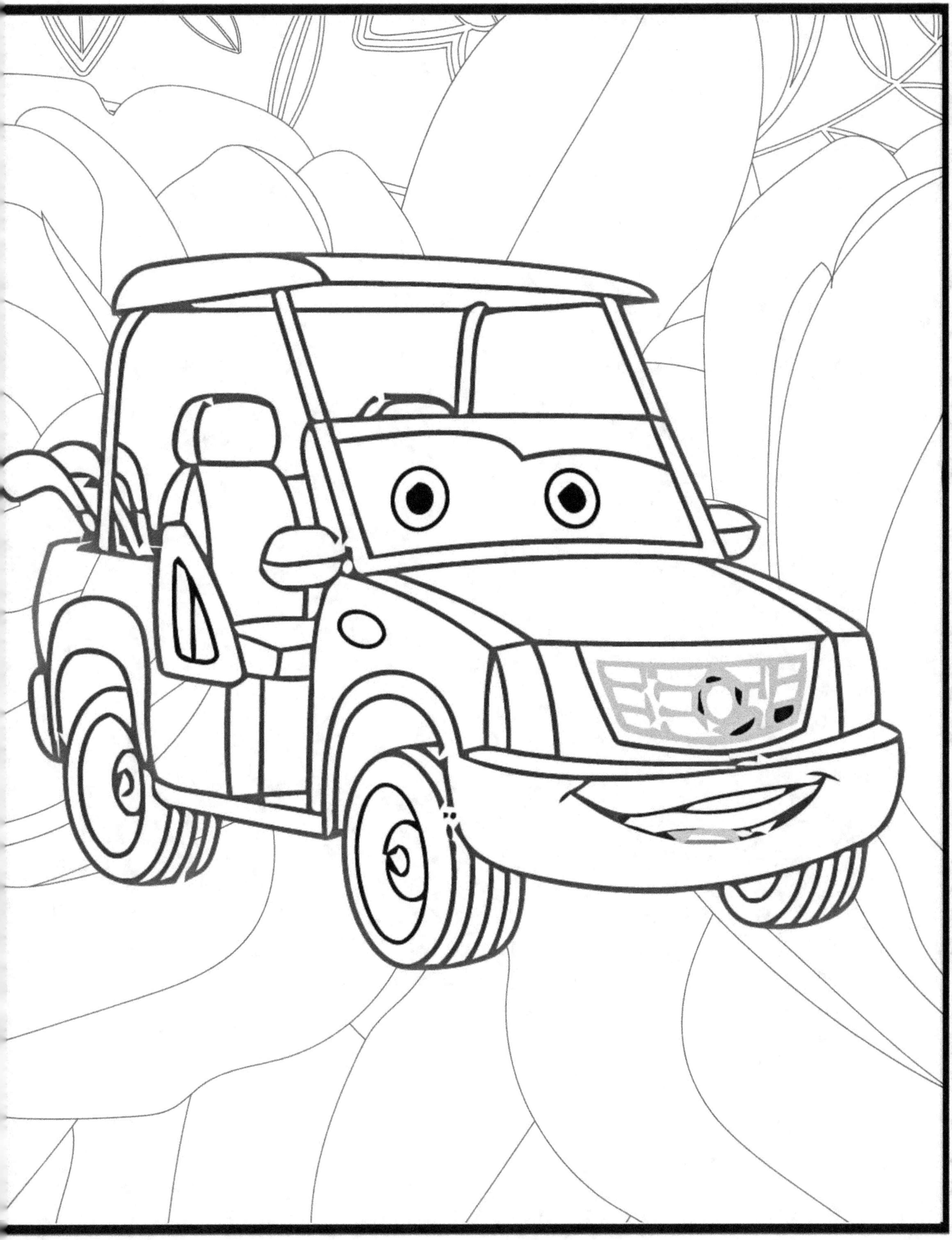

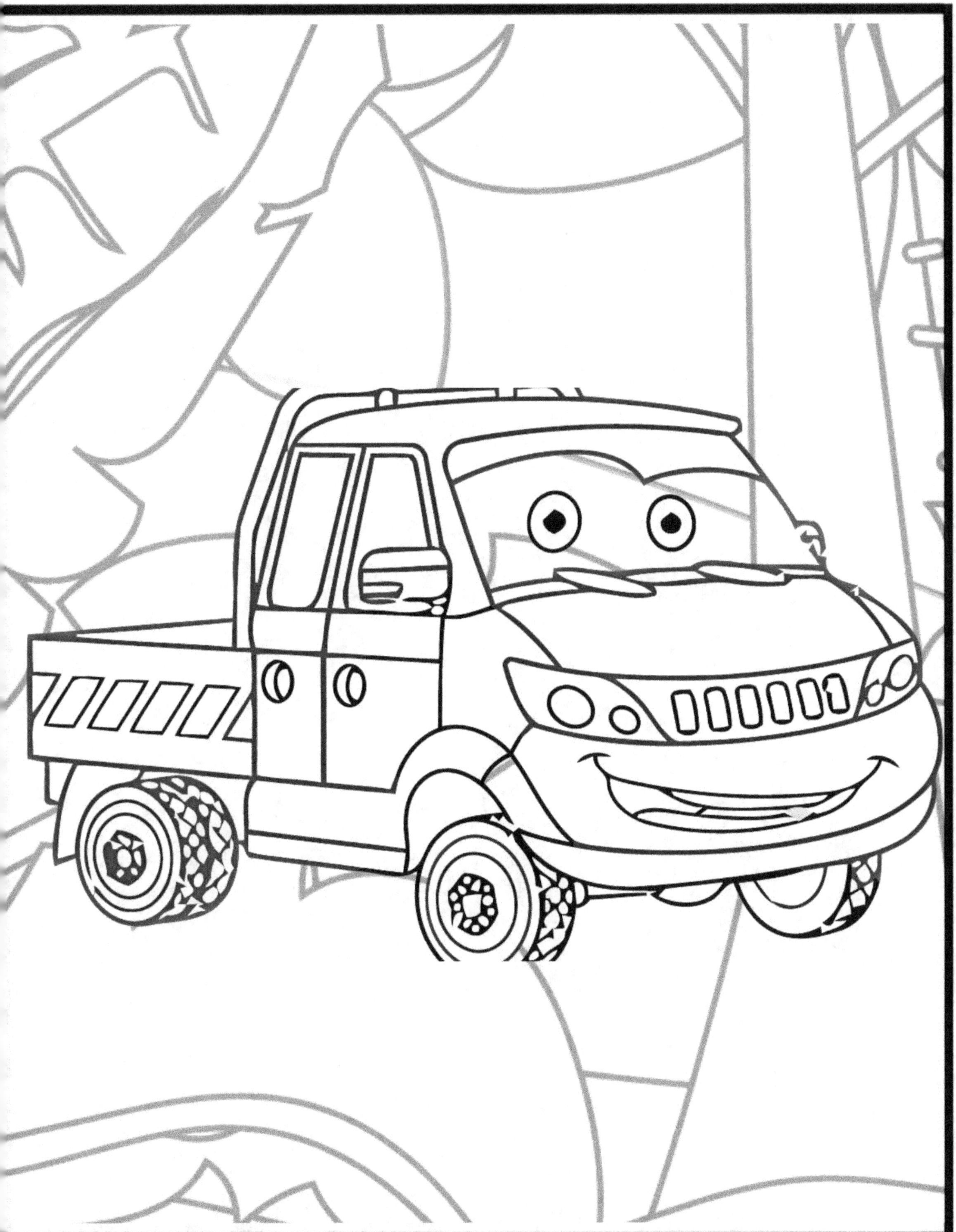

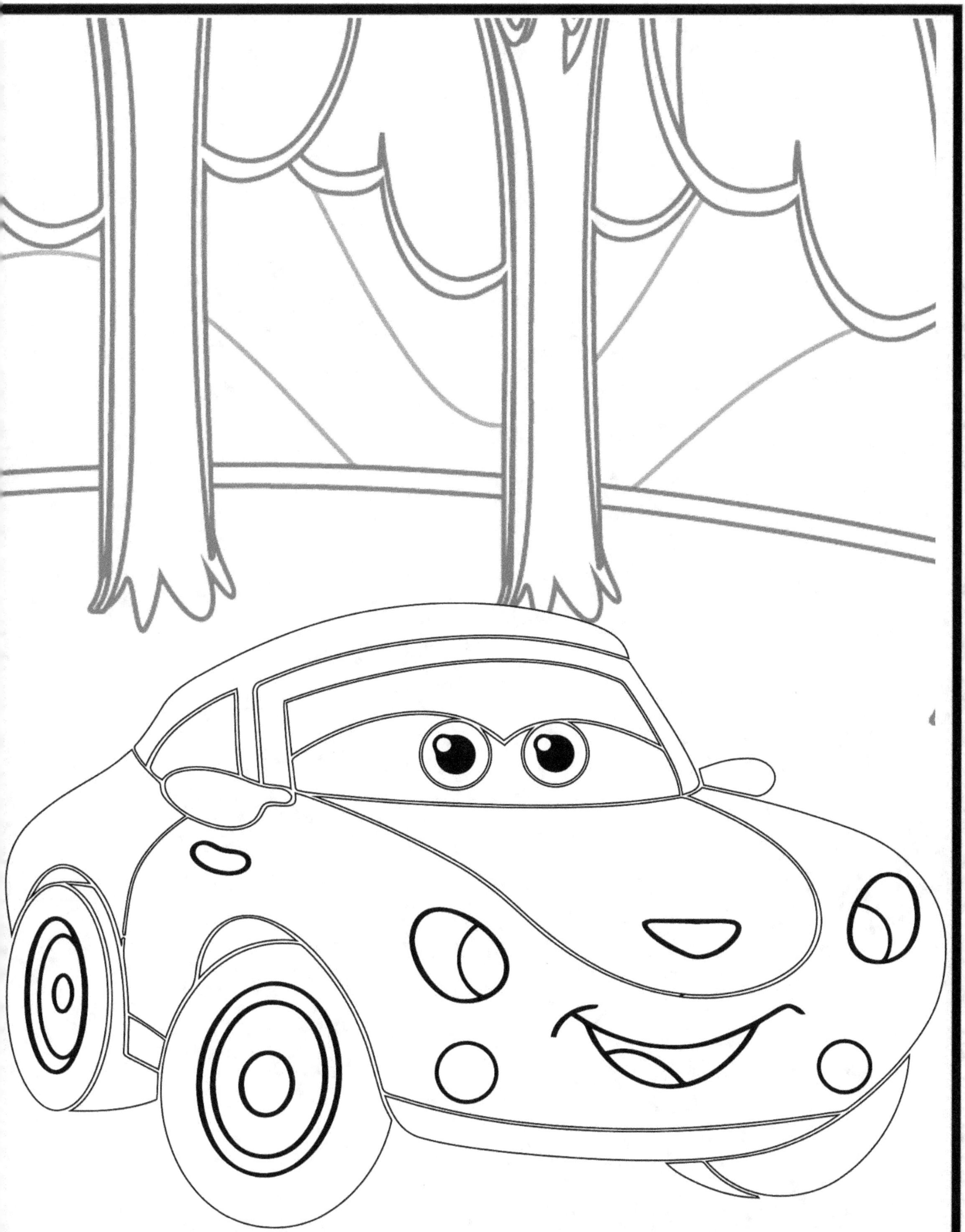

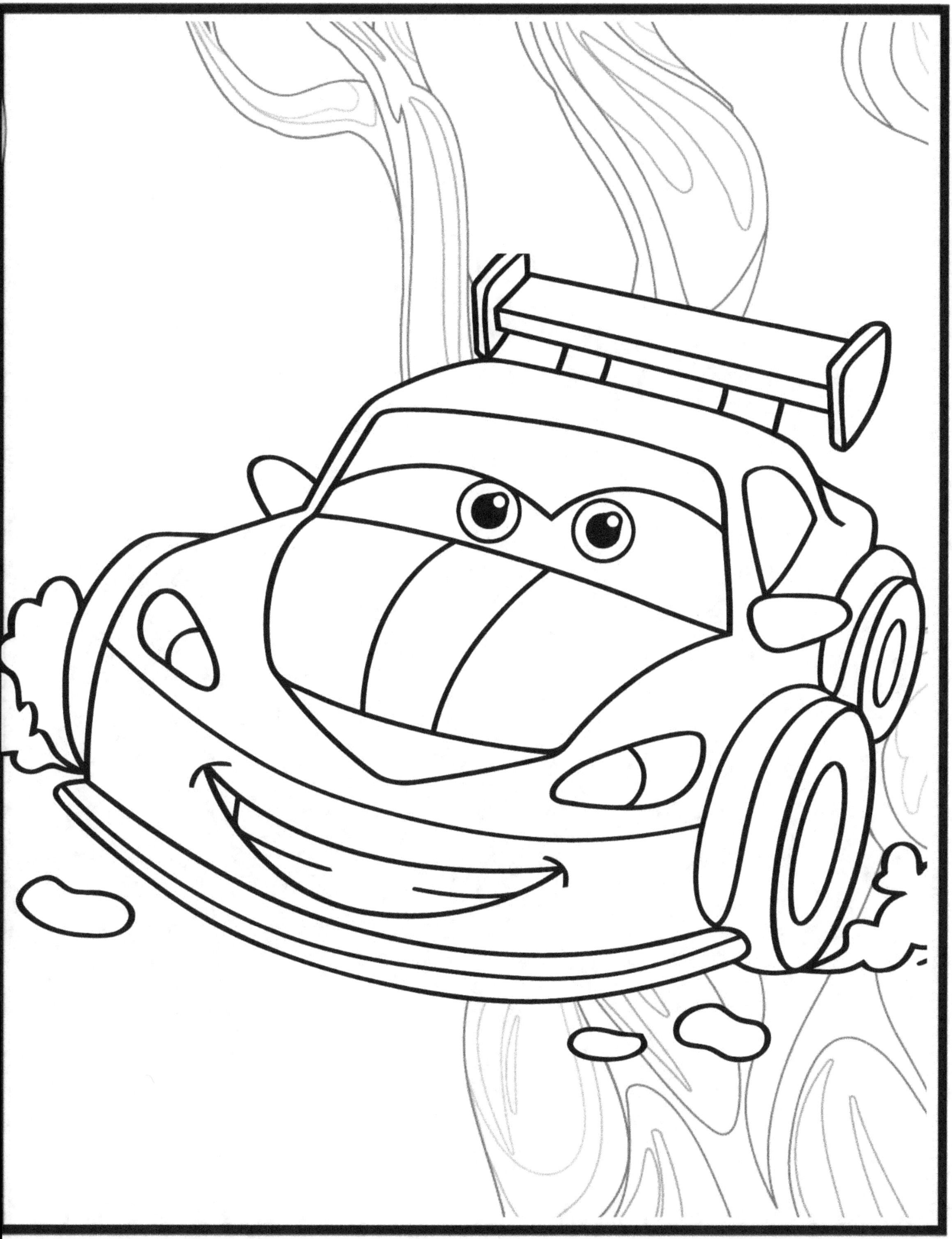

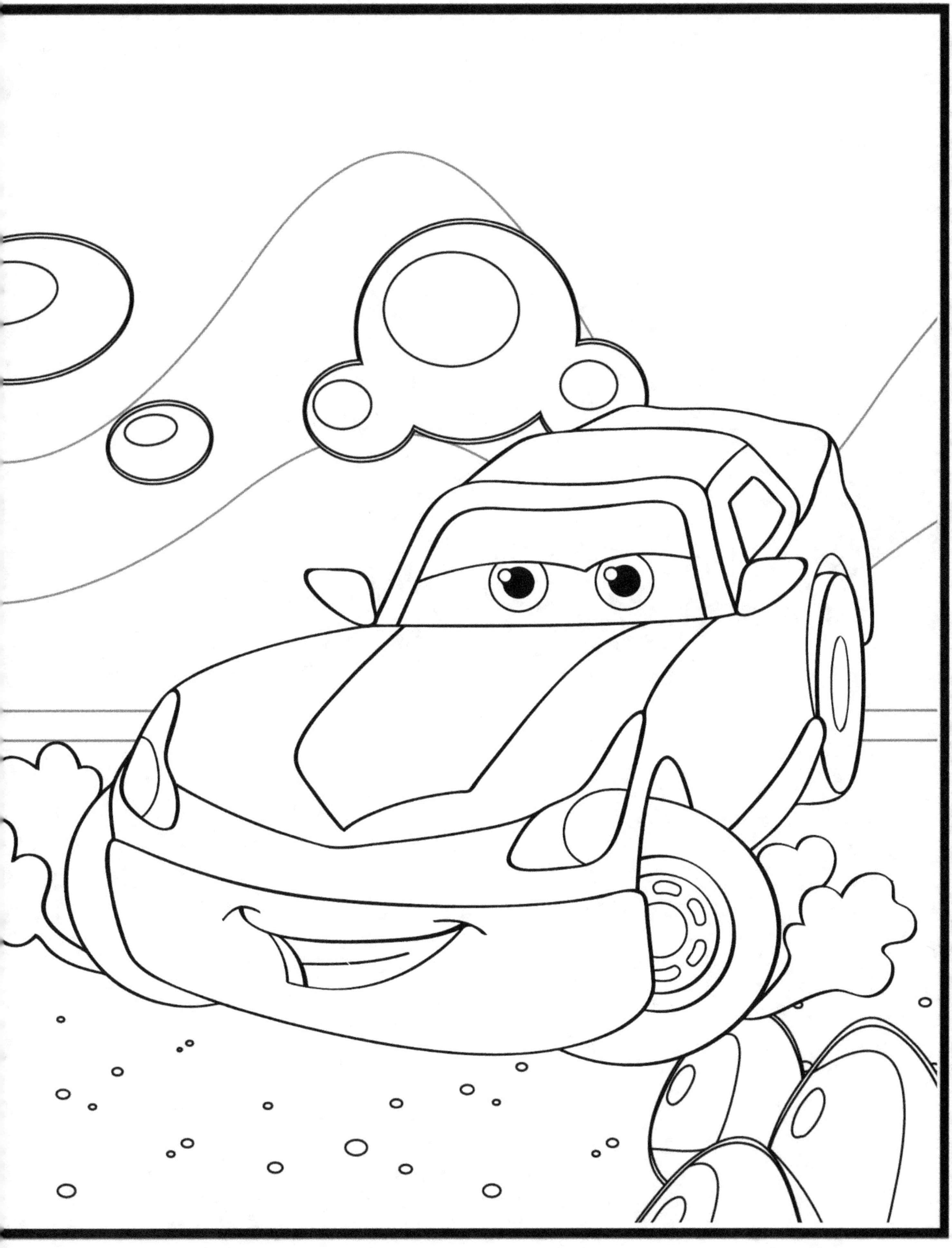

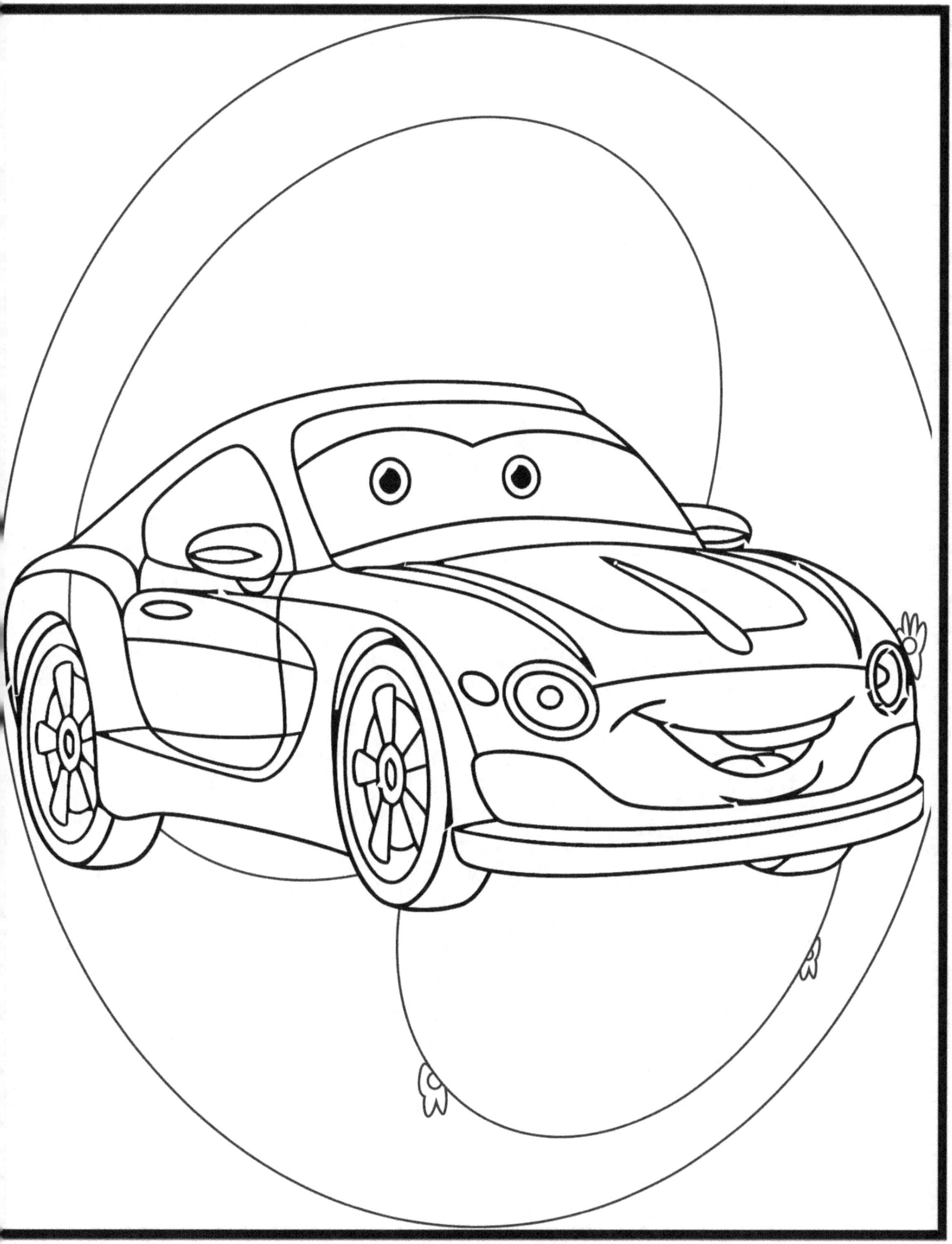

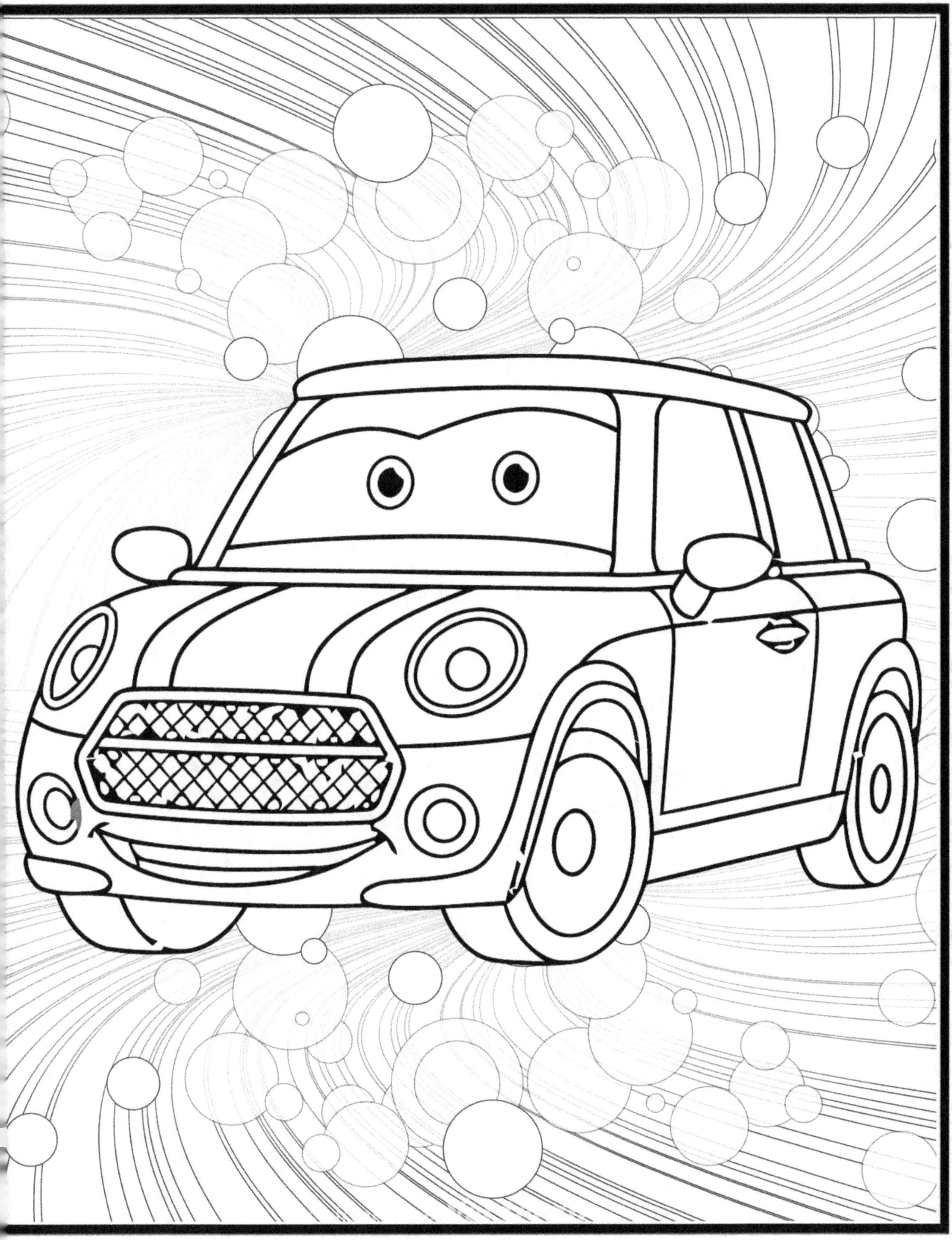

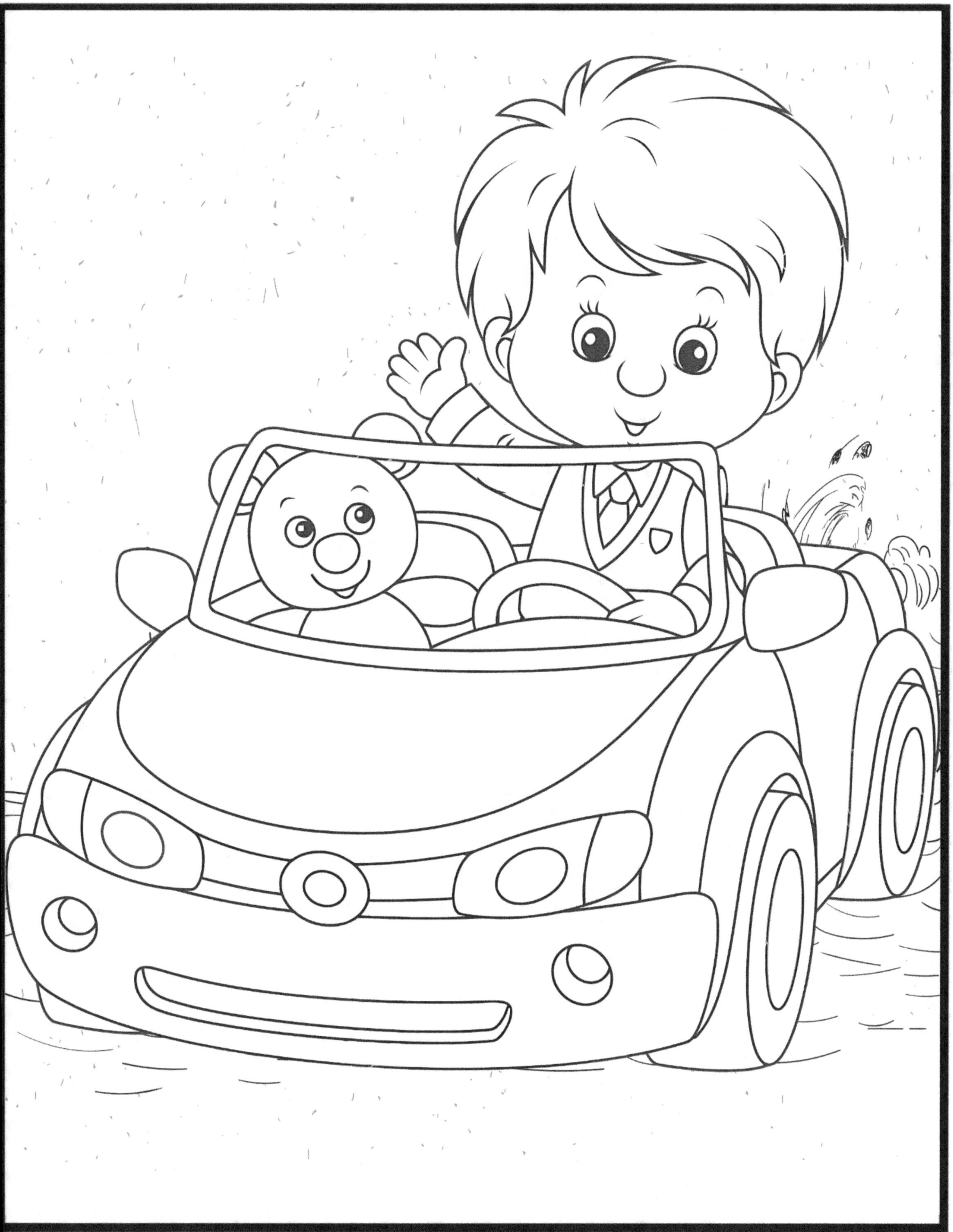

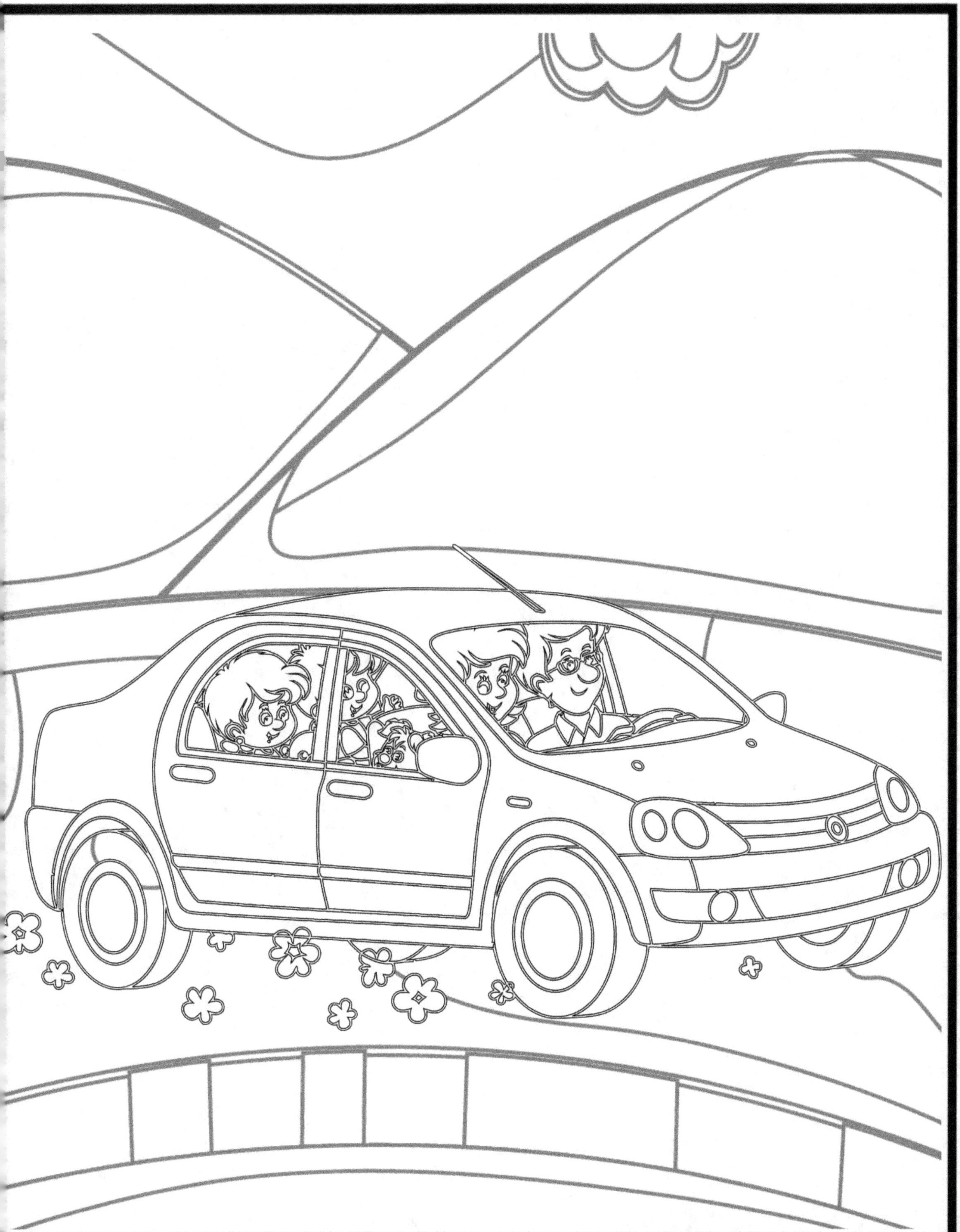

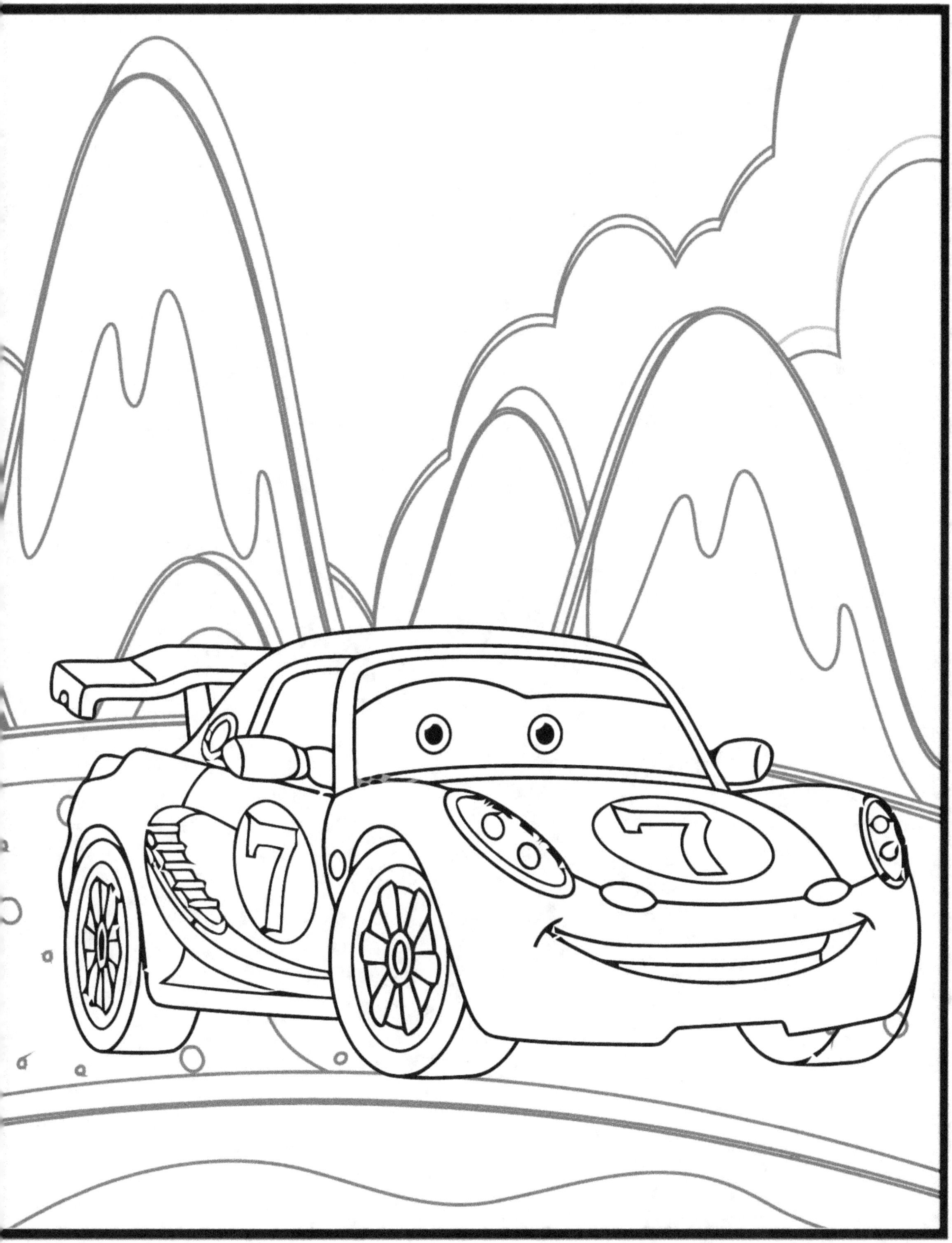

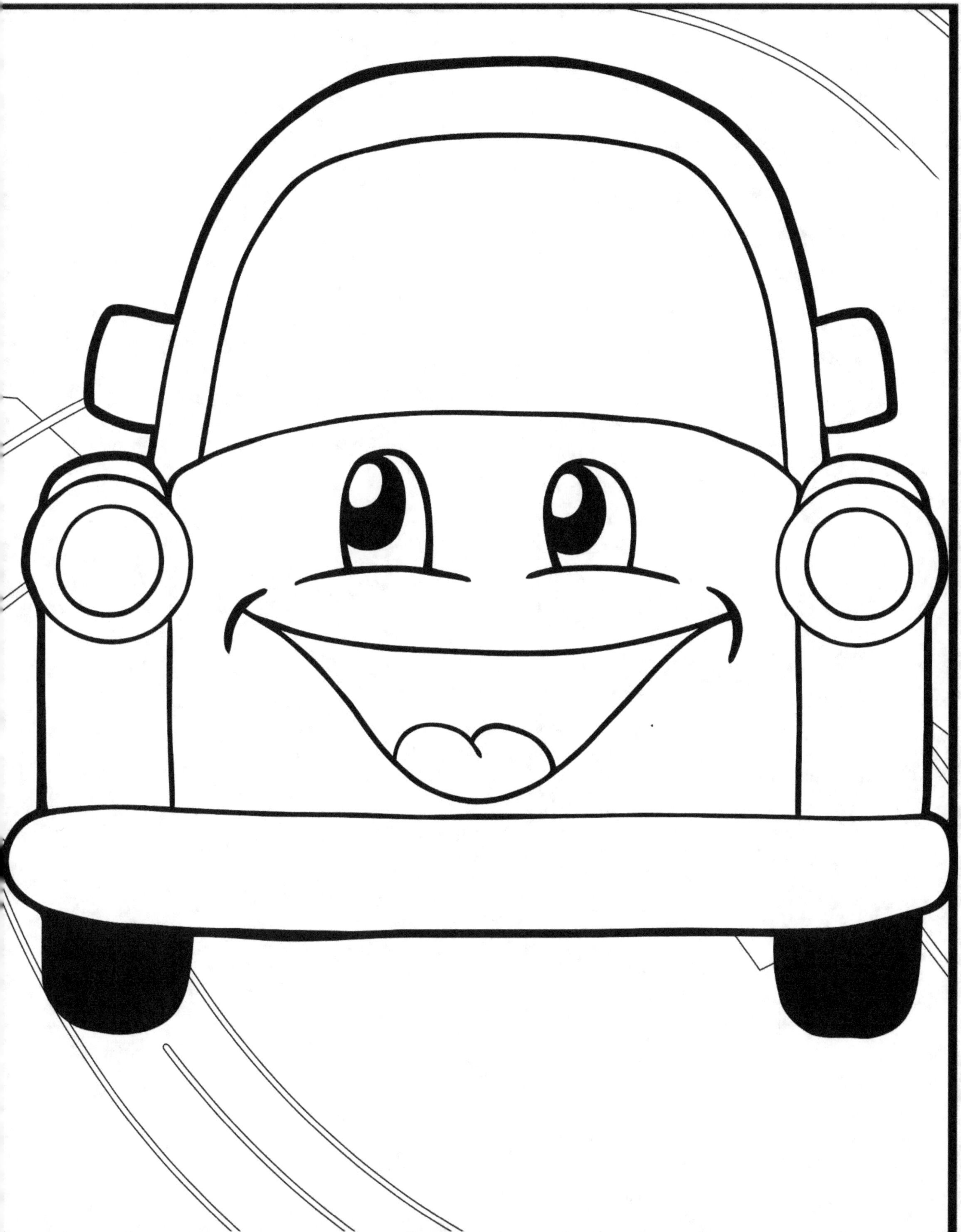

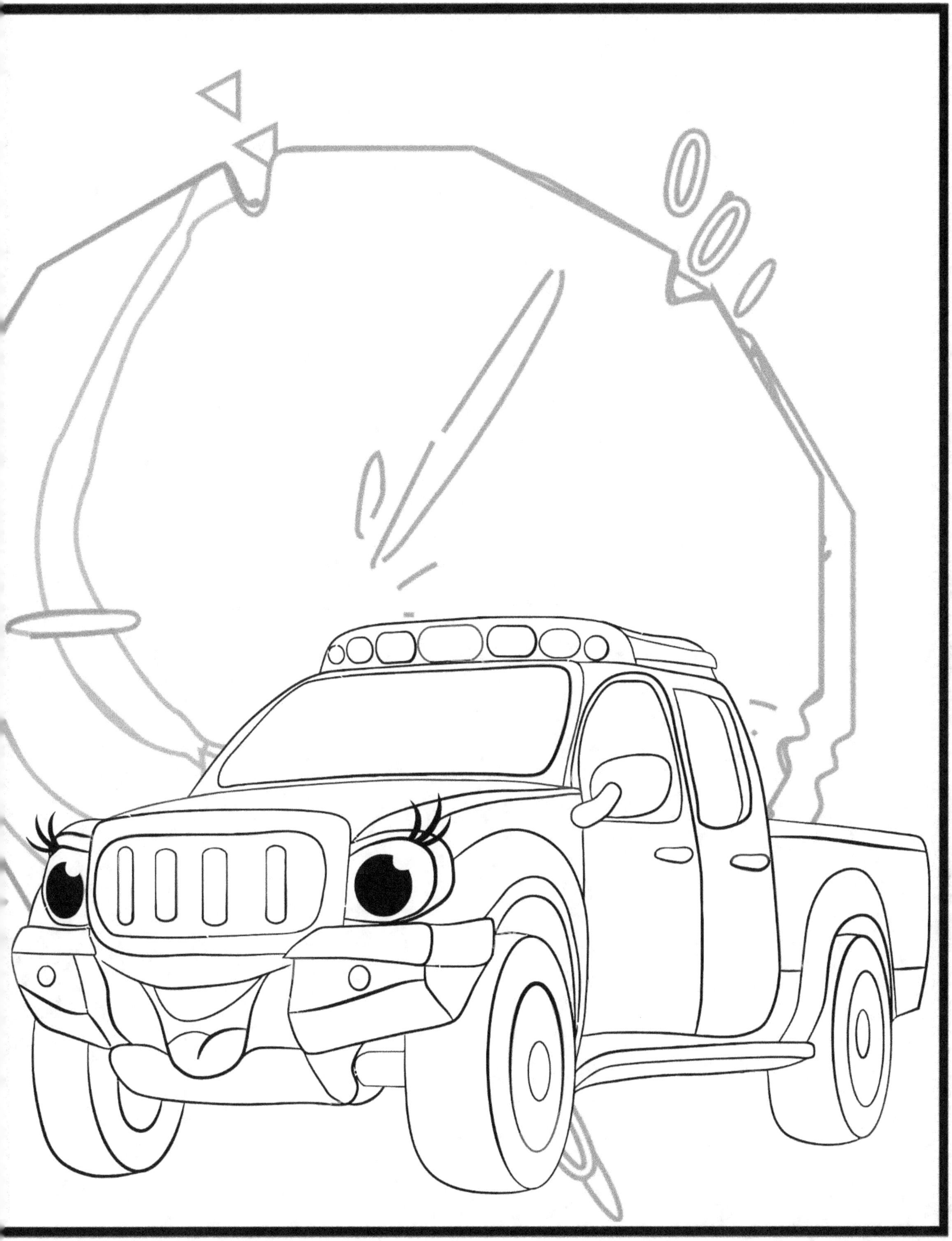

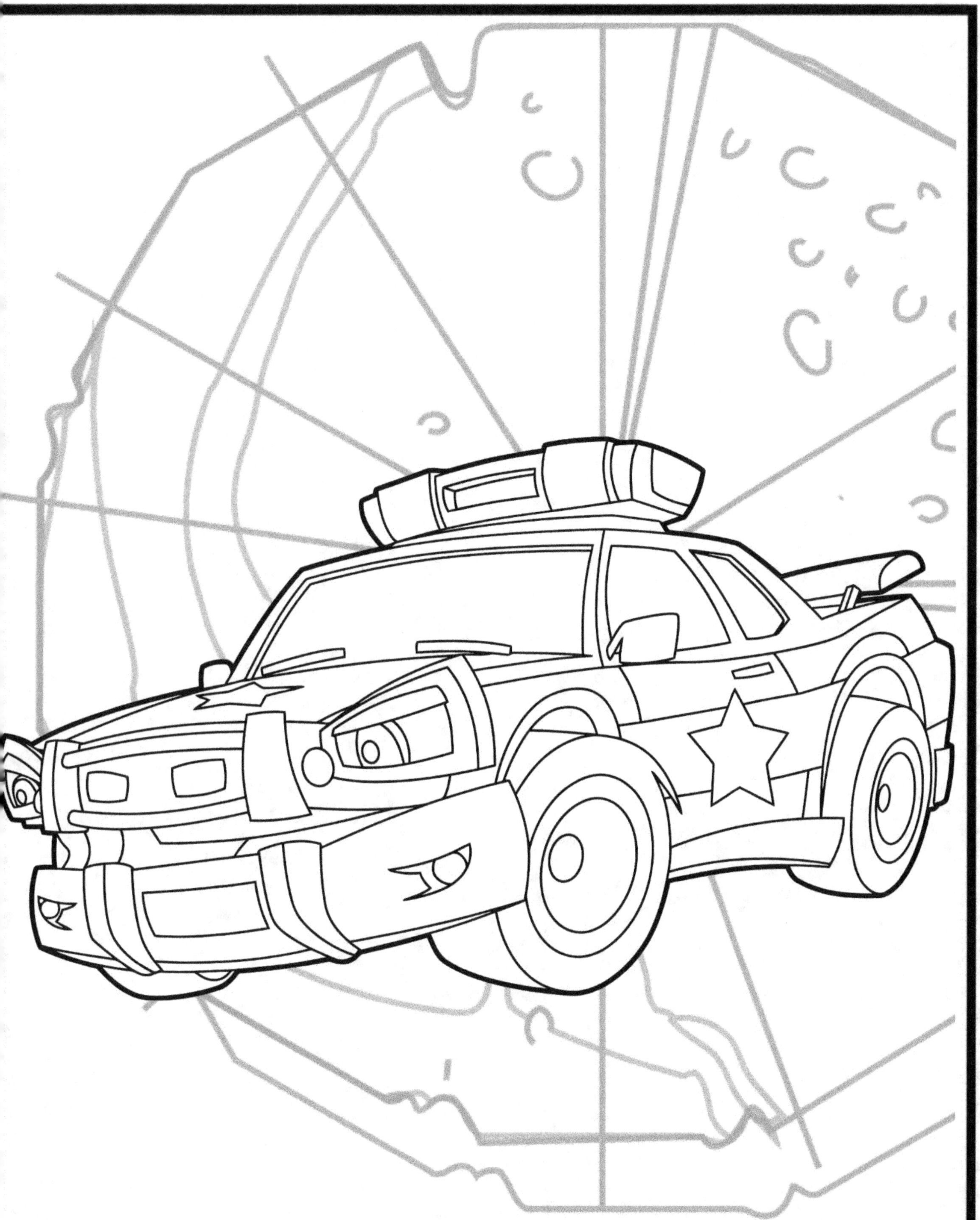

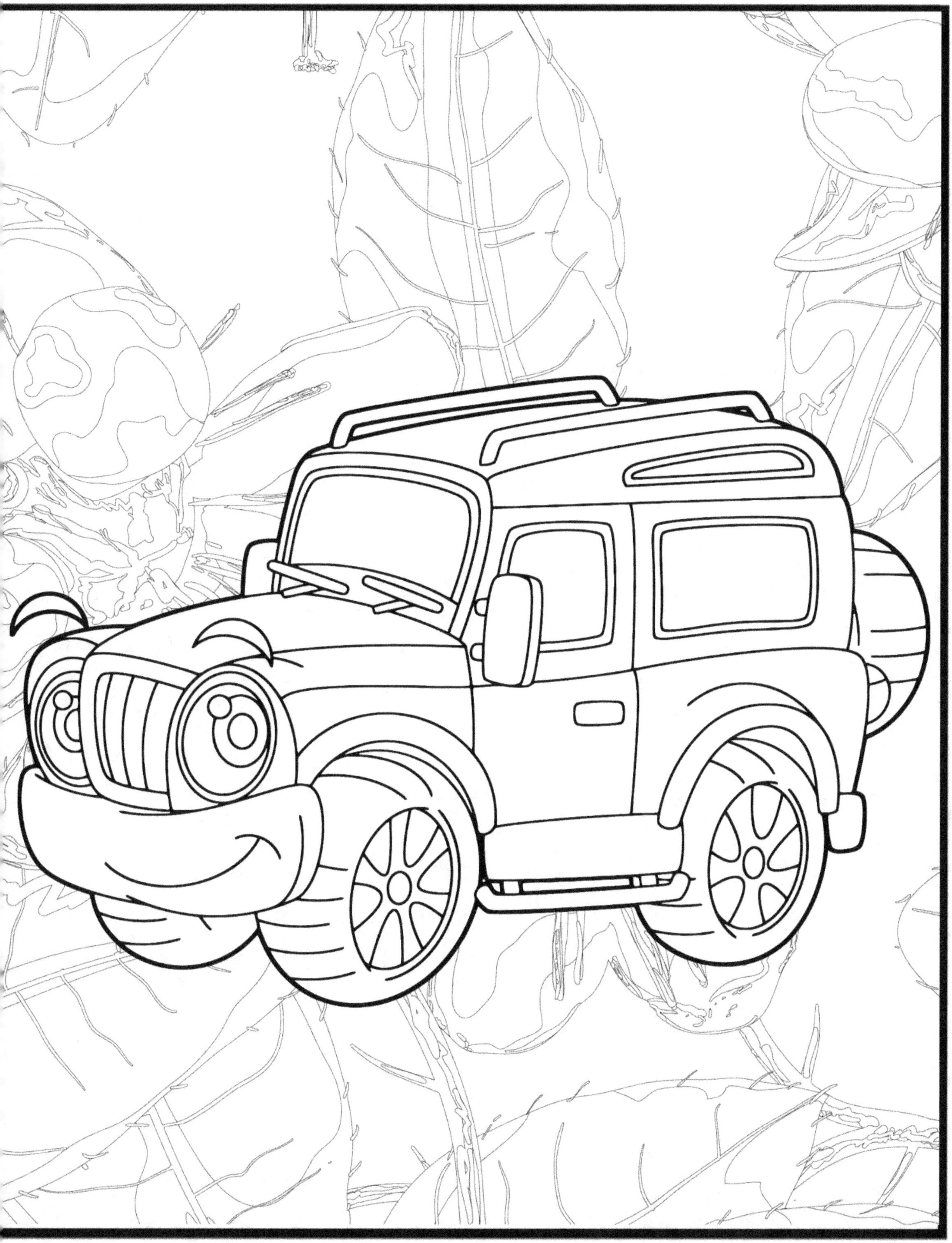

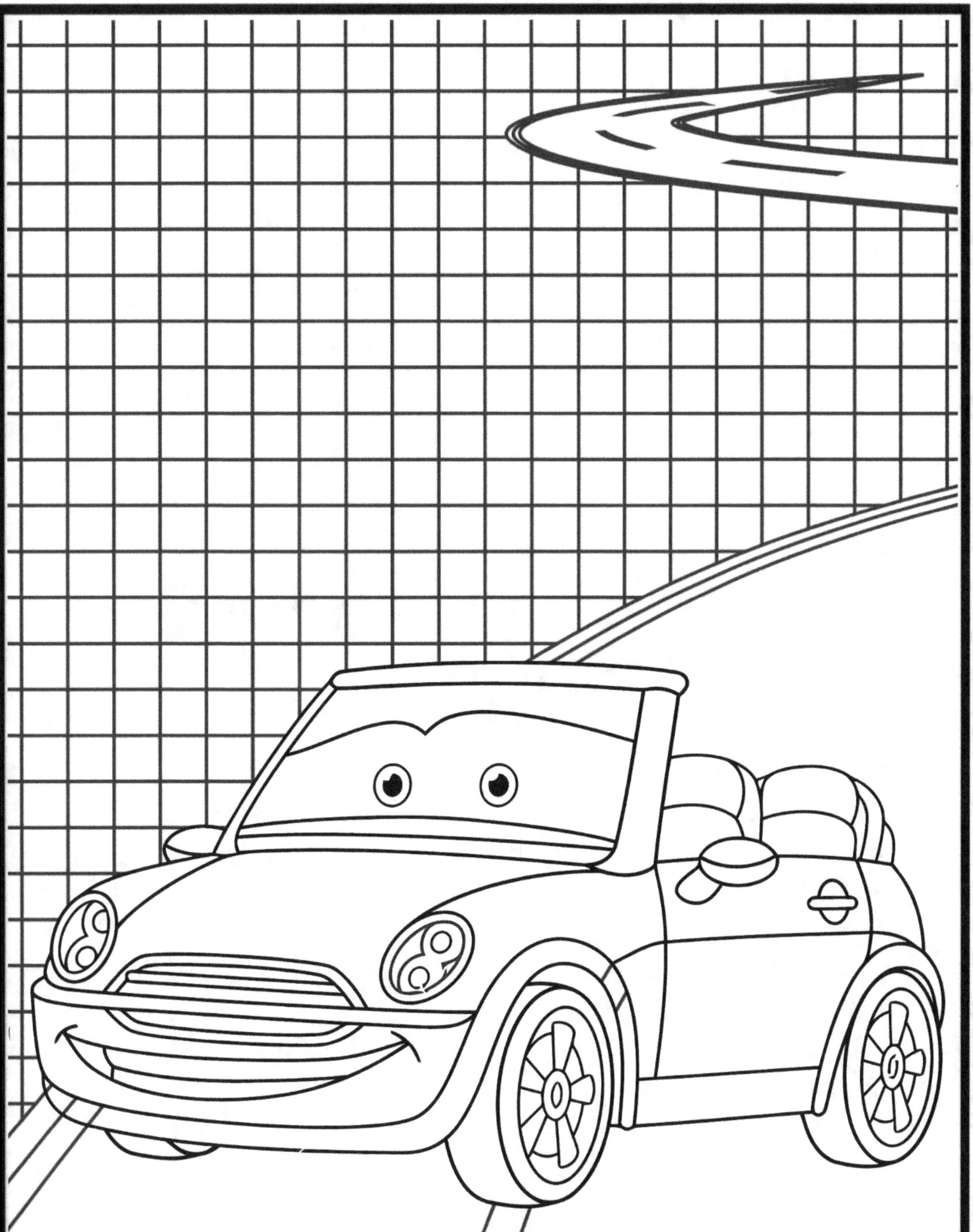

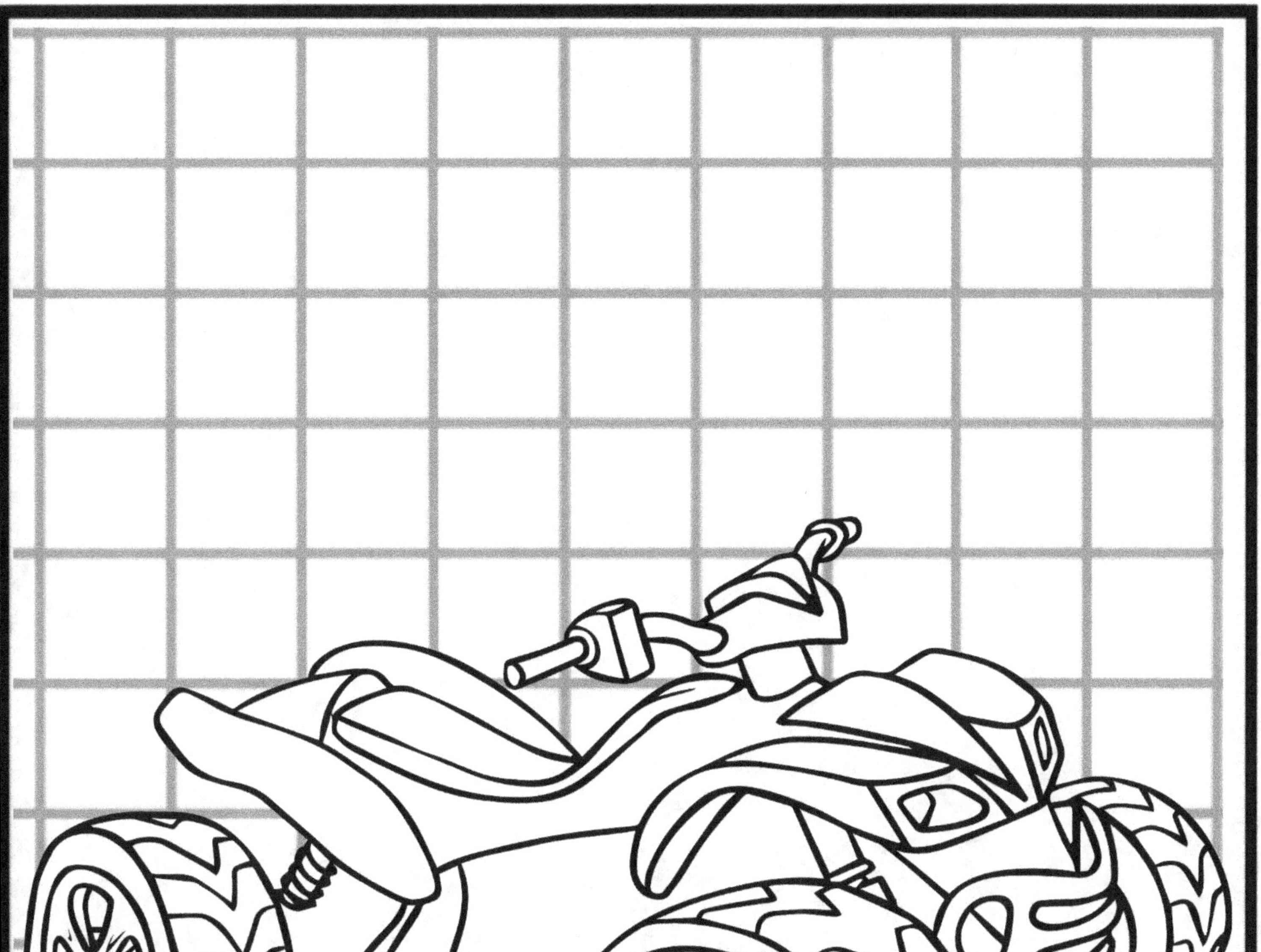

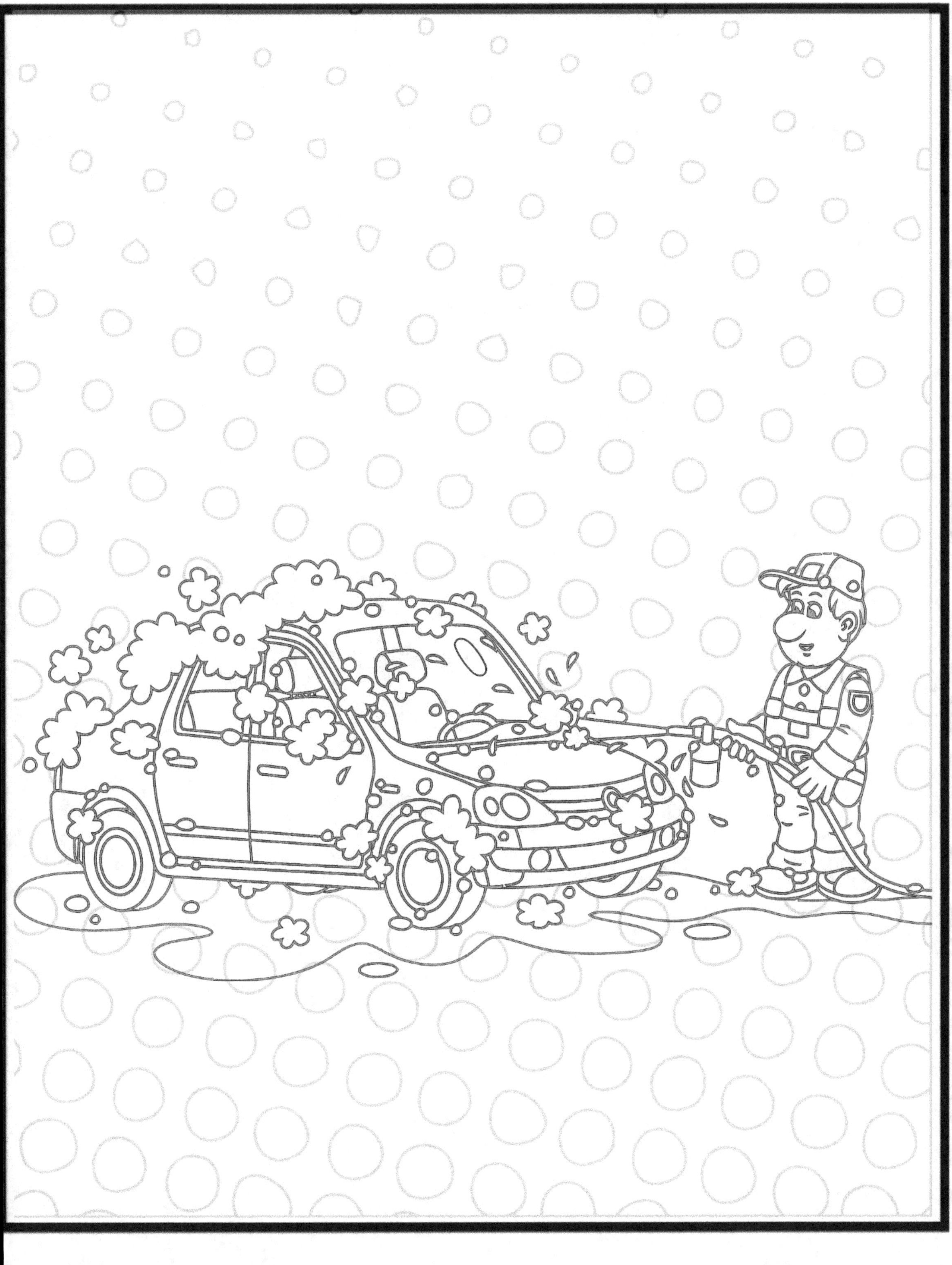

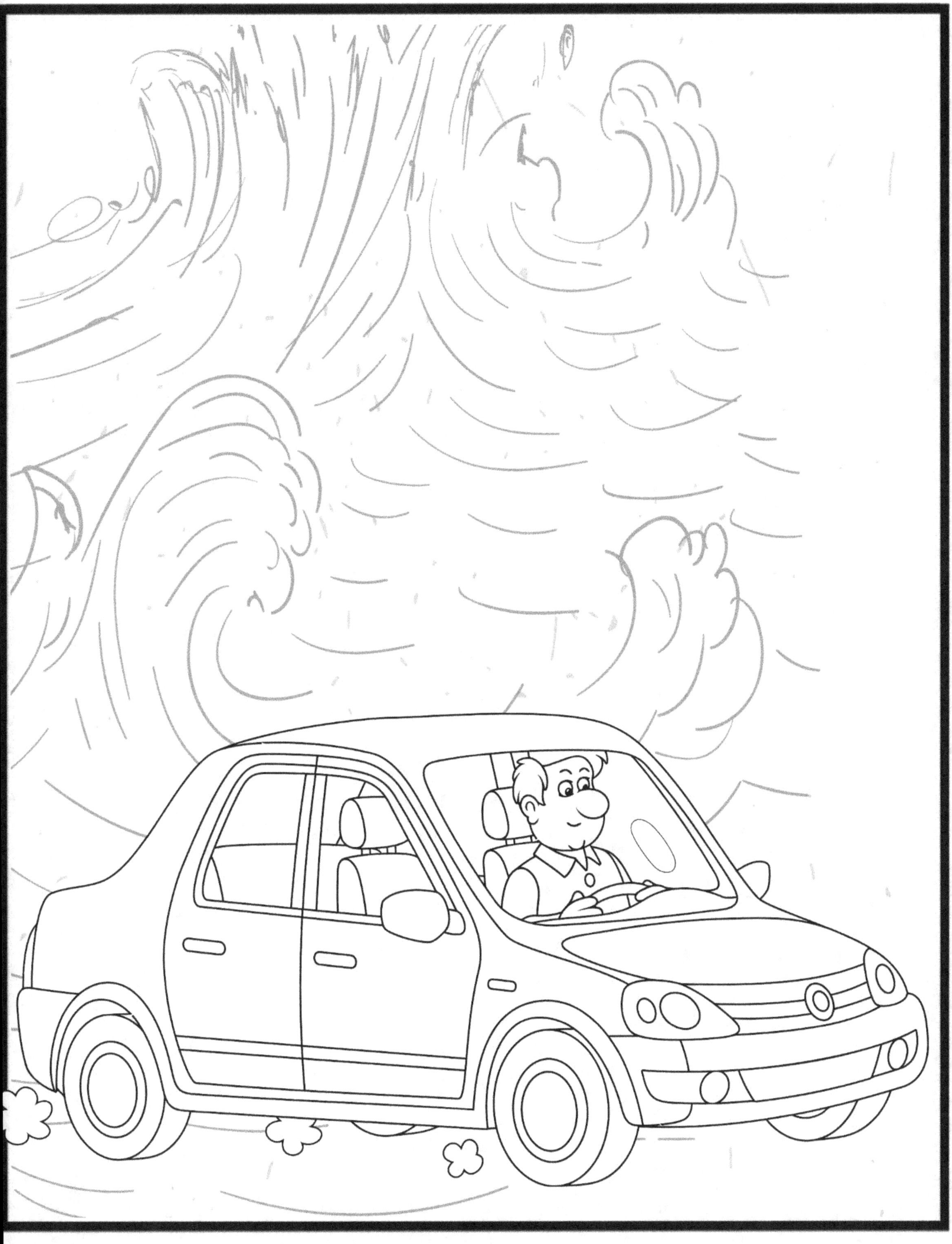

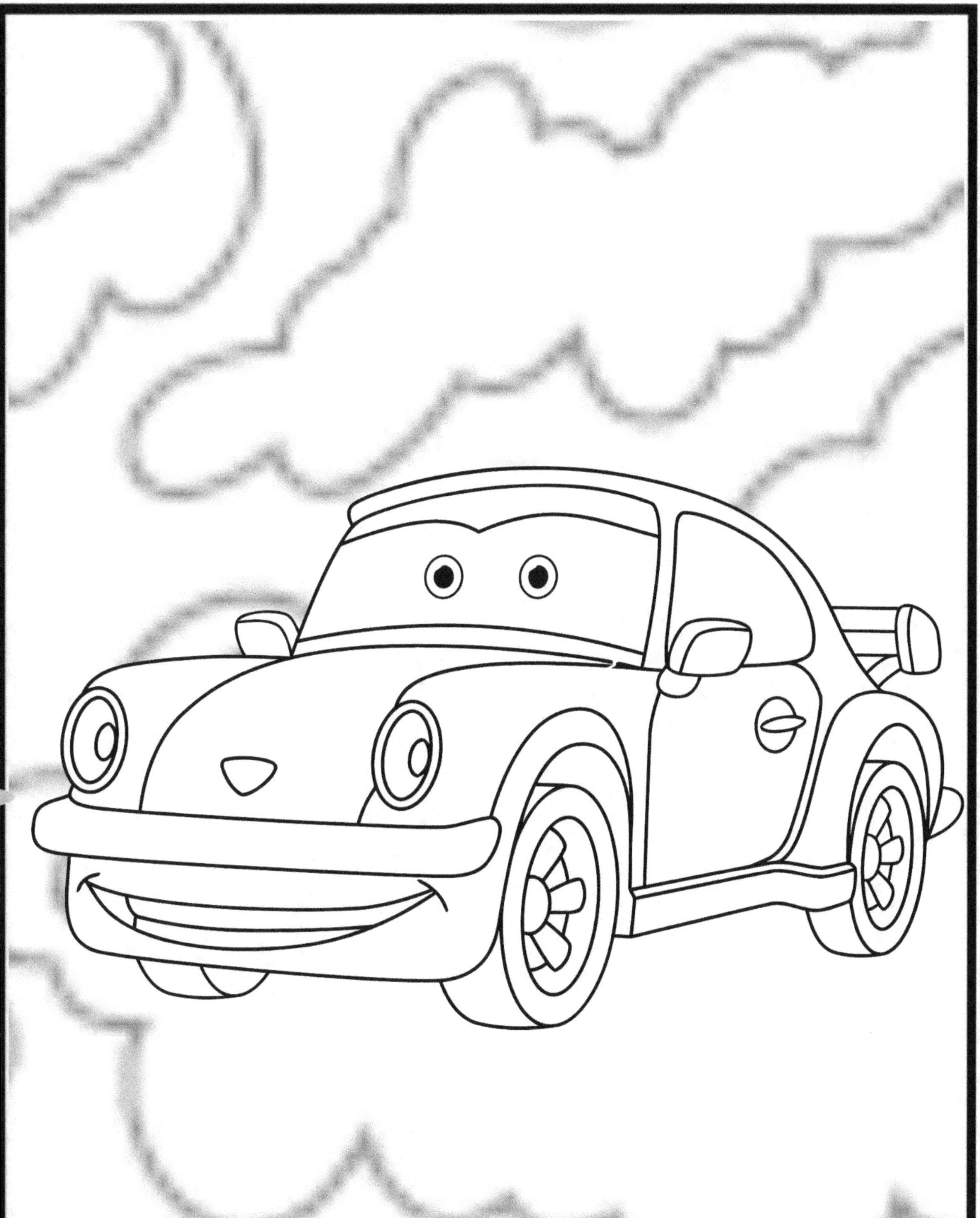

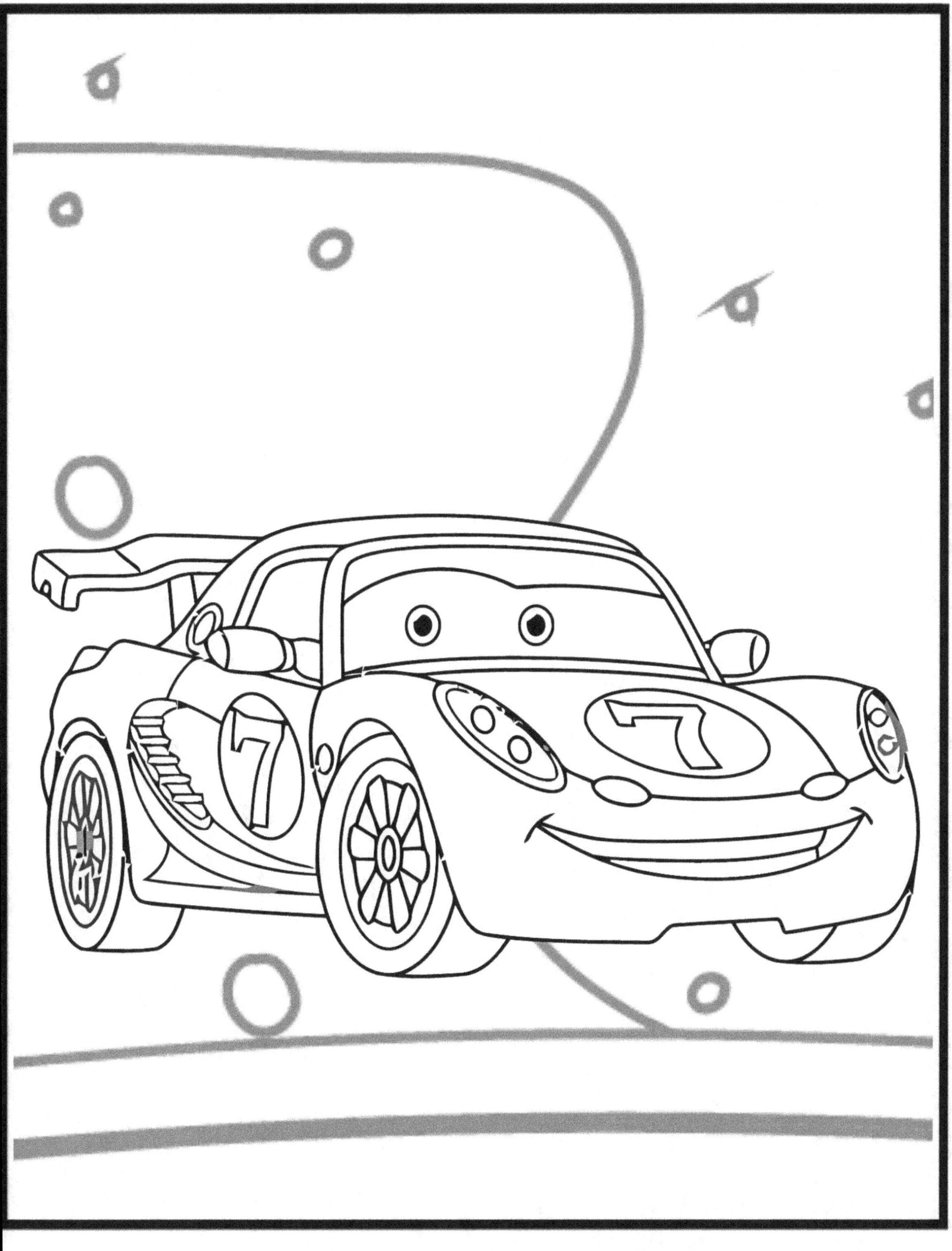

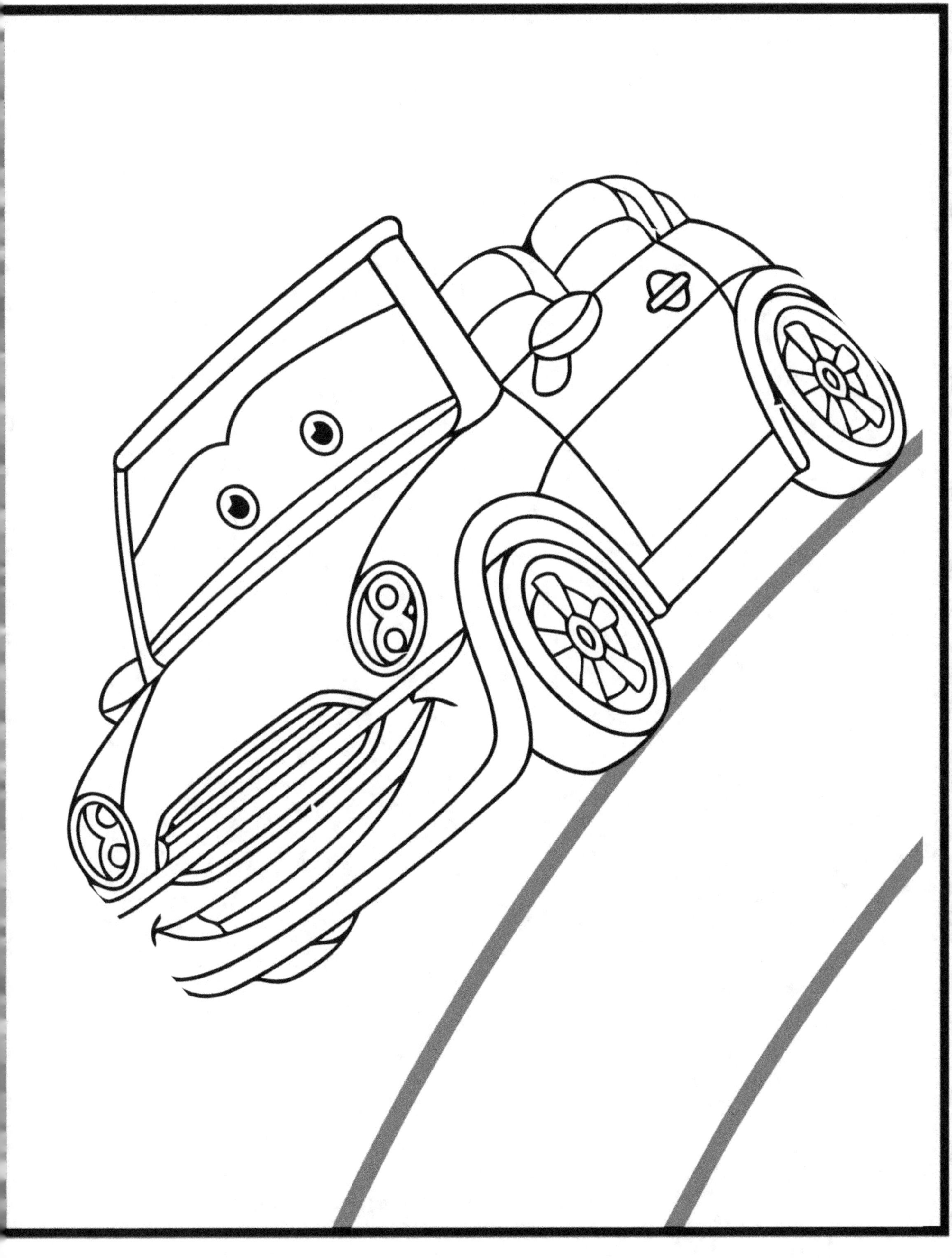

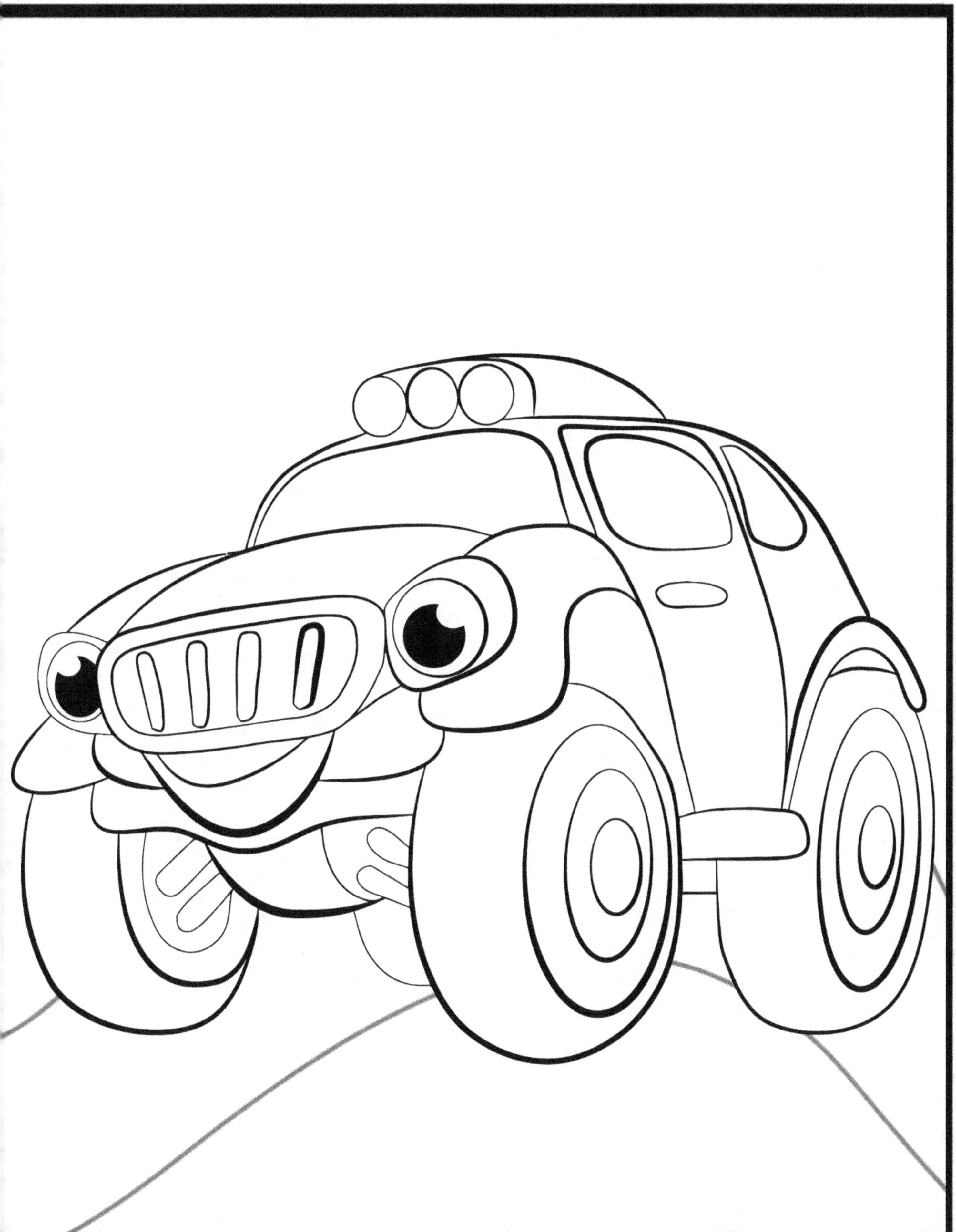

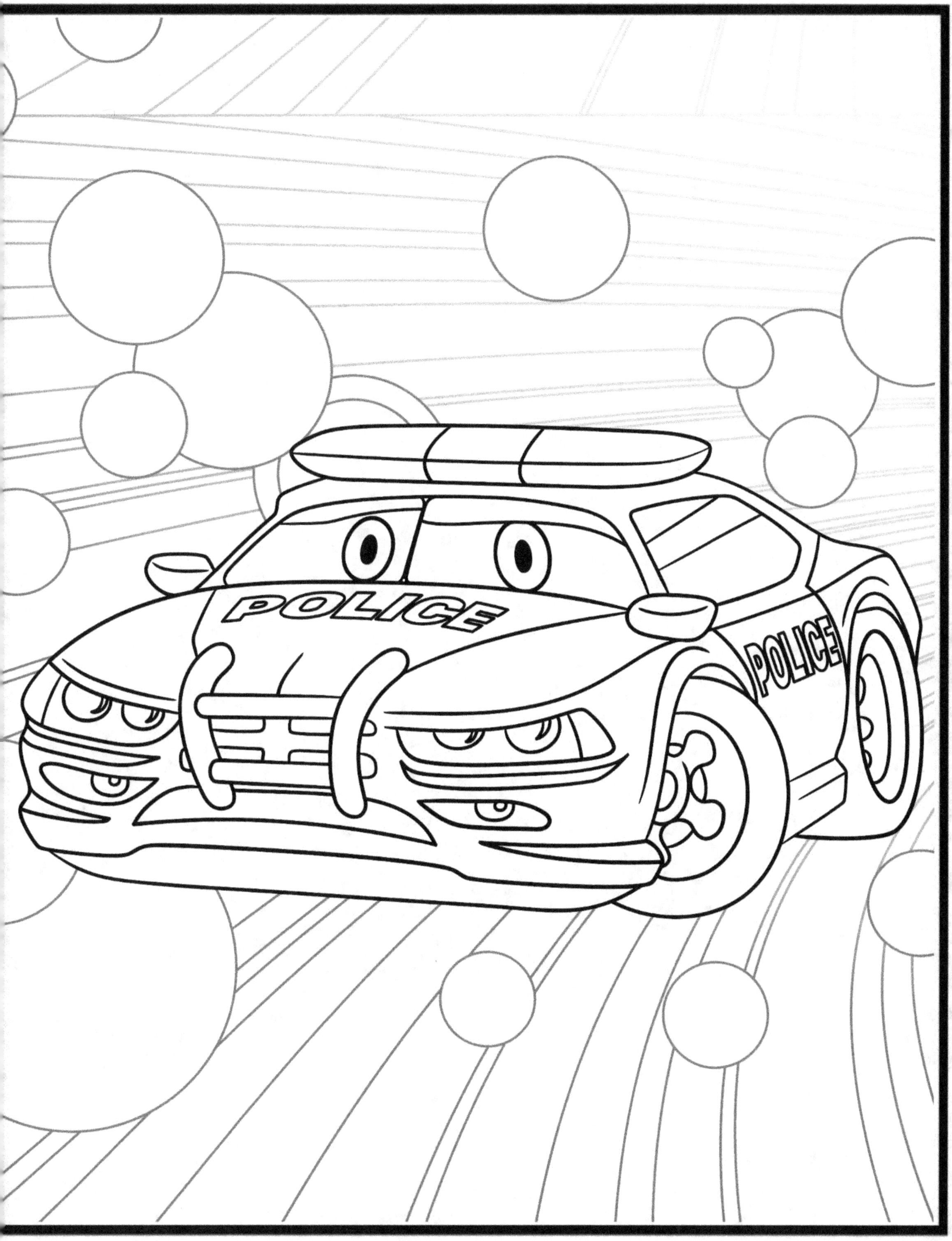
POLICE
POLICE

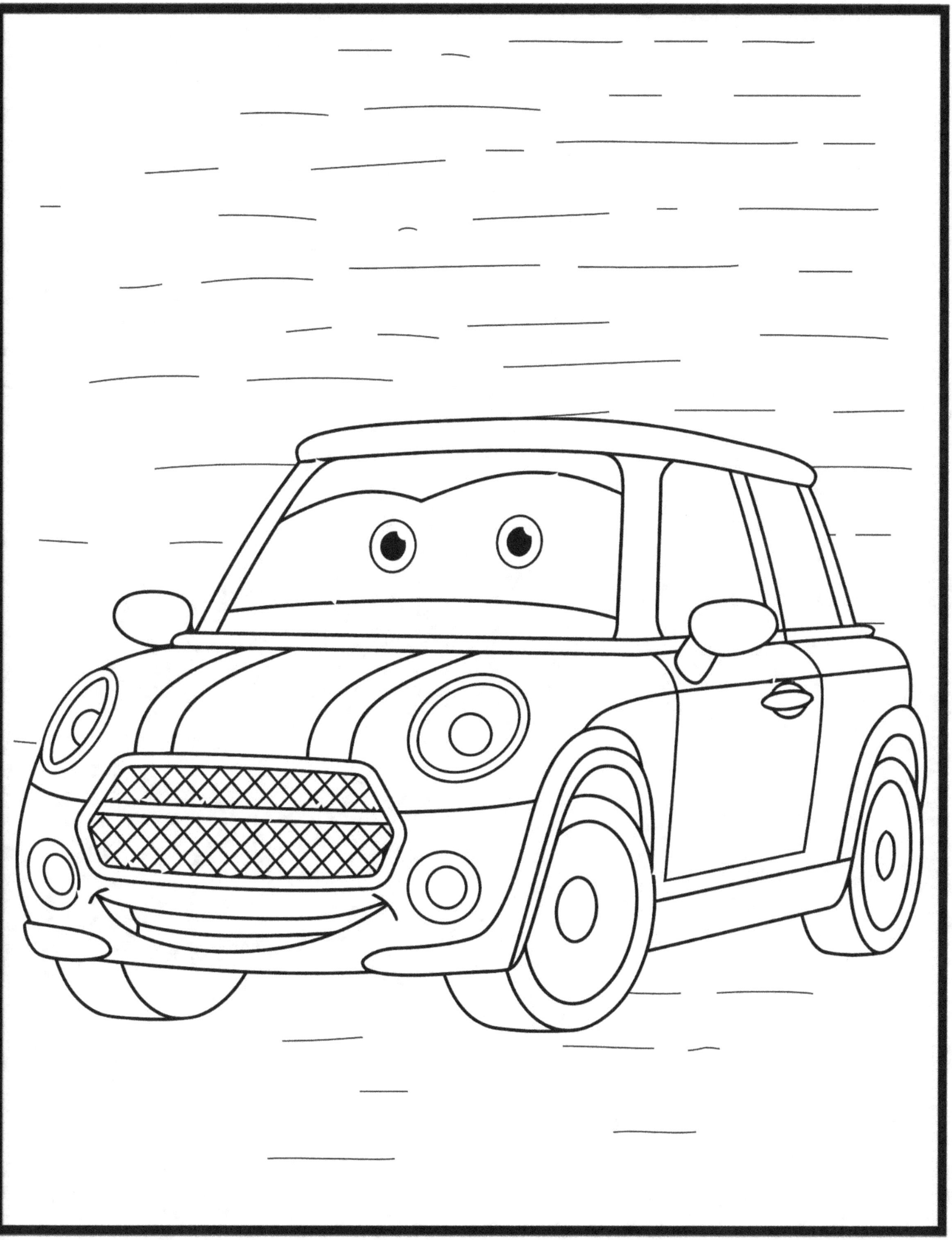

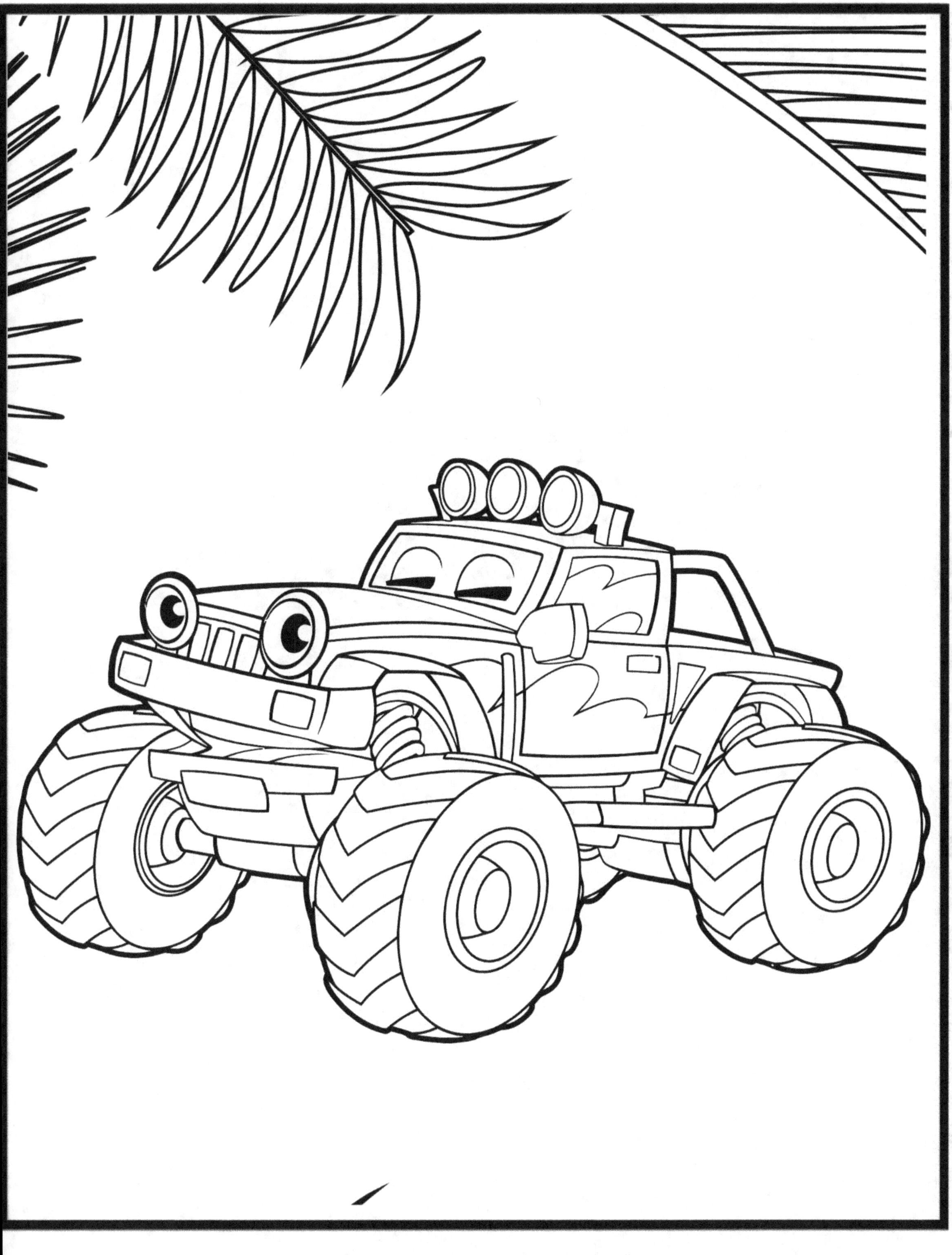

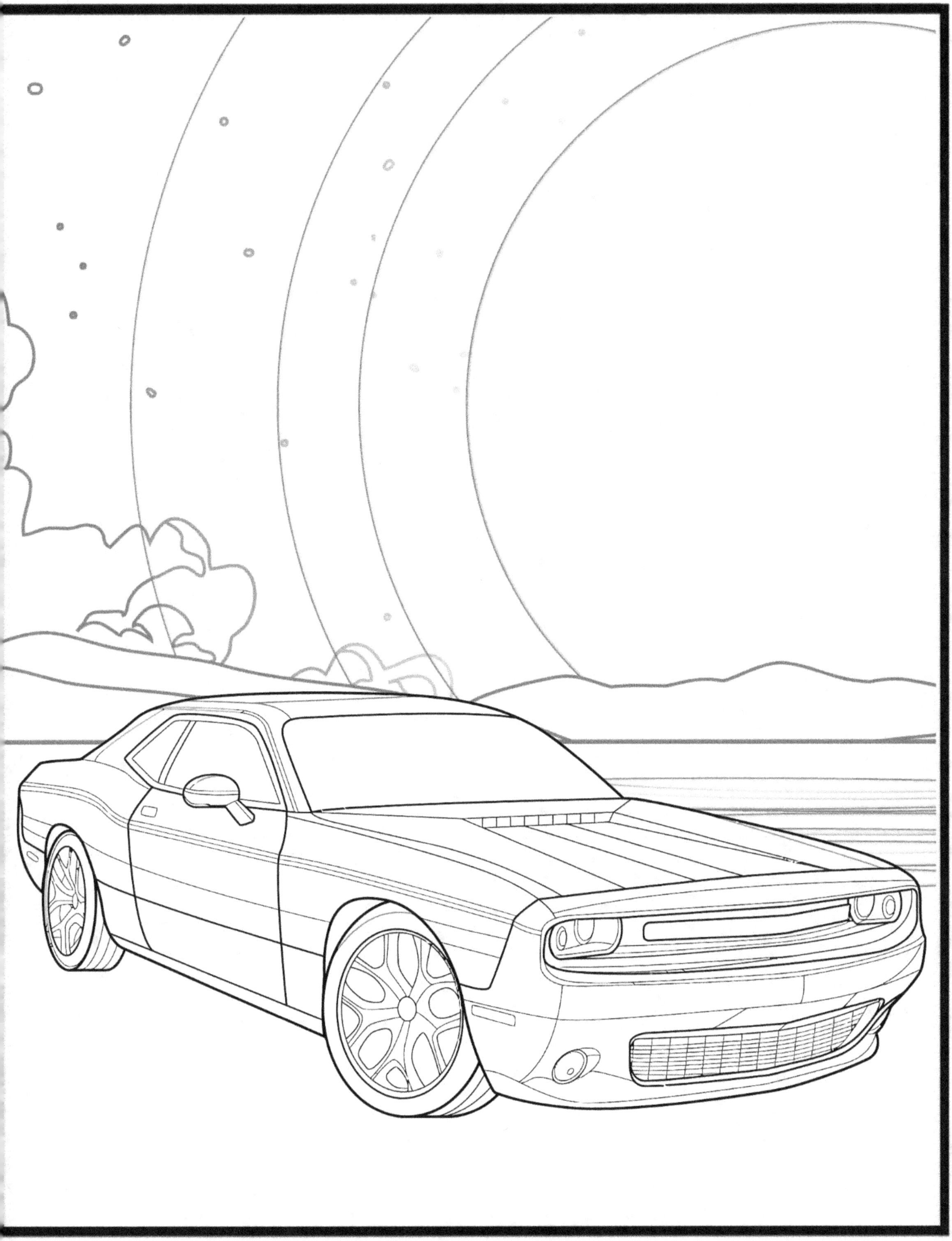

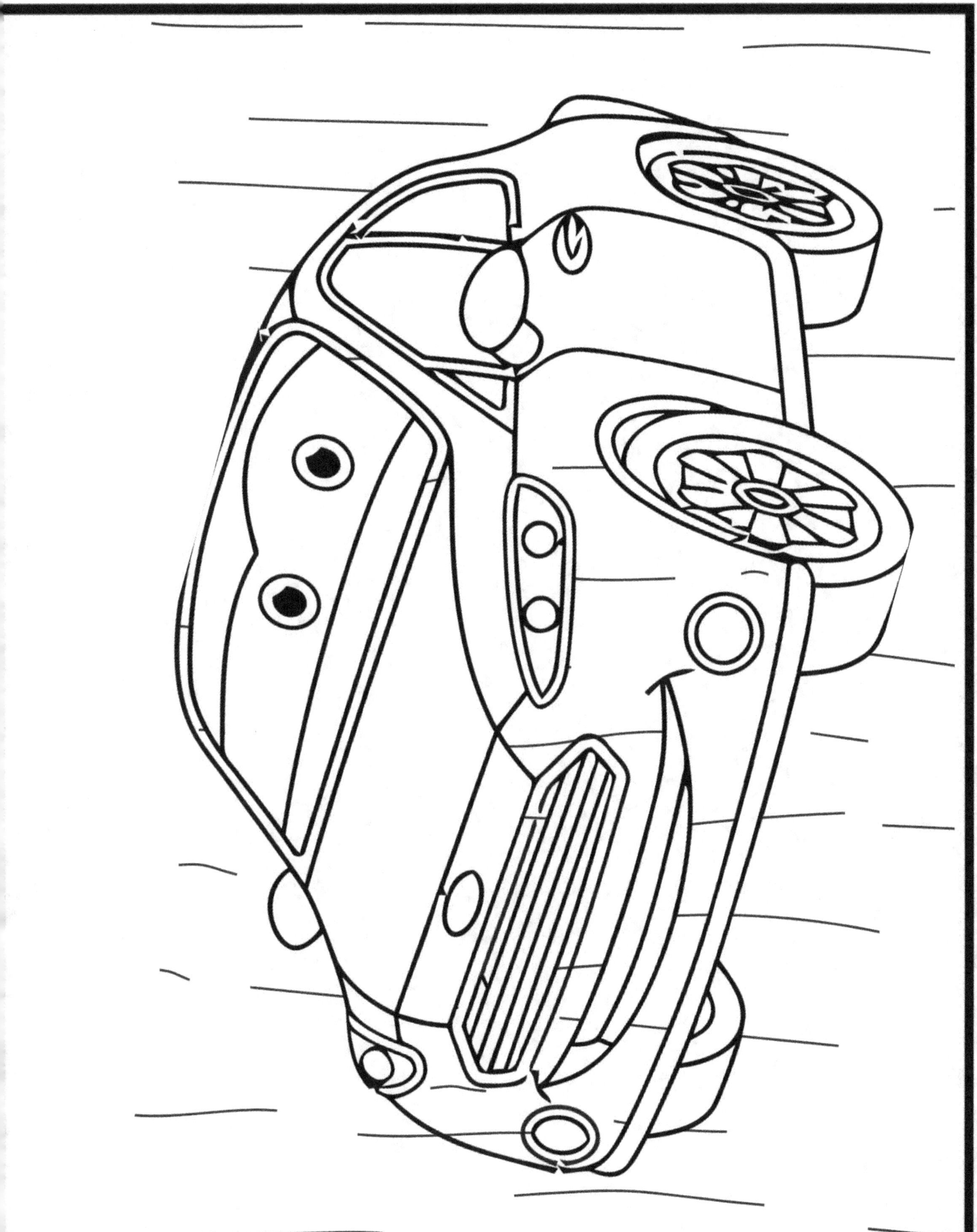

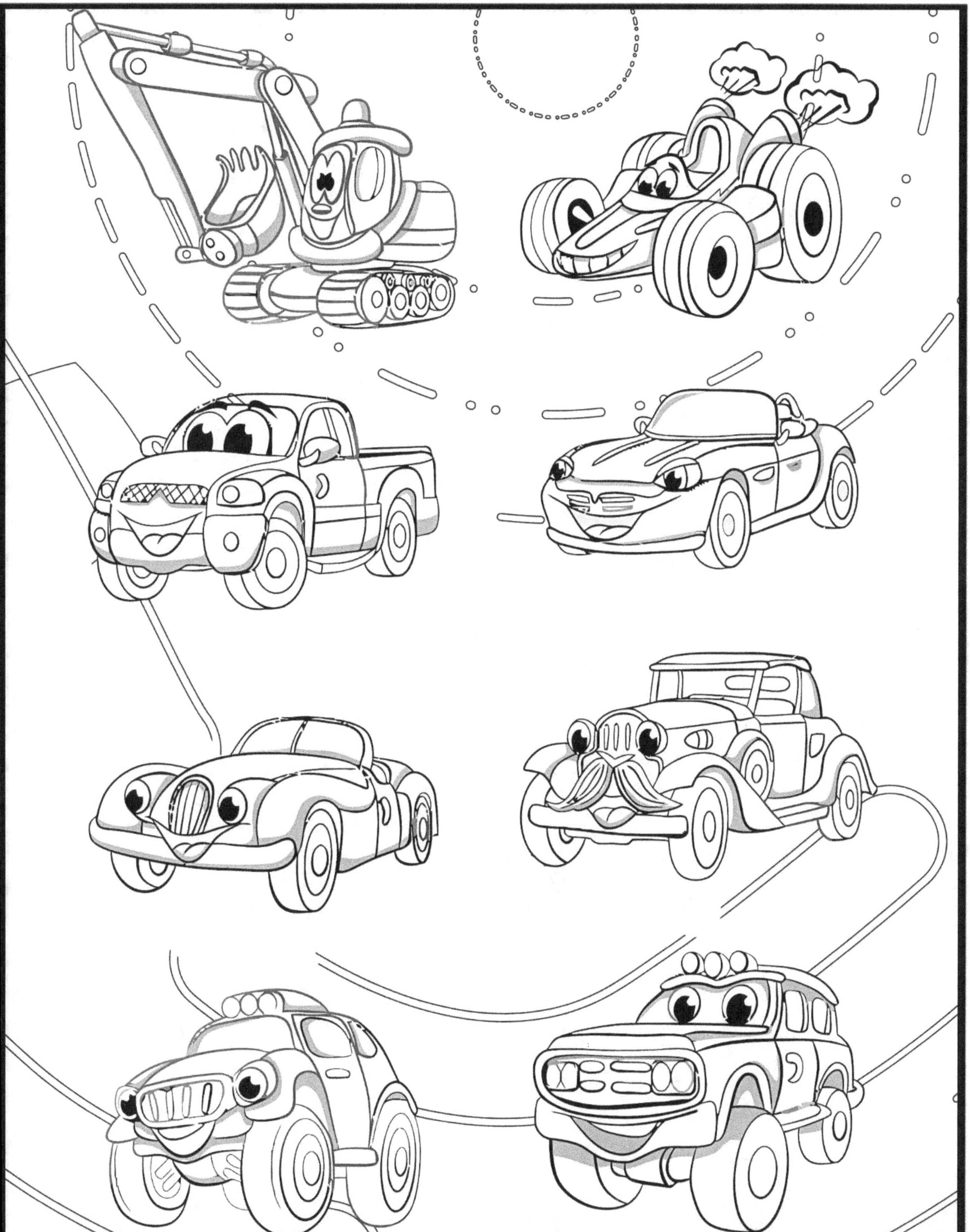

www.ingramcontent.com/pod-product-compliance
Lightning Source LLC
Chambersburg PA
CBHW080522220526
45465CB00006B/2563
* 9 7 9 8 7 4 9 7 3 2 6 0 3 *